THE WORKING LIFE

A Medieval Knight

THE WORKING LIFE

A Medieval Knight

JAMES BARTER

LUCENT BOOKS

An imprint of Thomson Gale, a part of The Thomson Corporation

THOMSON
™
GALE

Detroit • New York • San Francisco • San Diego • New Haven, Conn. • Waterville, Maine • London • Munich

For more information, contact
Lucent Books
27500 Drake Rd.
Farmington Hills, MI 48331-3535
Or you can visit our Internet site at http://www.gale.com

LIBRARY OF CONGRESS CATALOGING-IN-PUBLICATION DATA

Barter, James, 1946–
  A medieval knight / by James Barter.
    p. cm. — (The working life series).
Includes bibliographical references and index
  ISBN 1-59018-580-3 (Hardcover : alk. paper.)
  1. Knights and knighthood—Juvenile literature. 2. Civilization, Medieval—Juvenile literature. I. Title. II. Series.
  CR4513.B37 2005
  940.1'088'355—dc22
                                   2004019389

CONTENTS

FOREWORD

"The strongest bond of human sympathy outside the family relations should be one uniting all working people of all nations and tongues and kindreds."

Abraham Lincoln, 1864

Work is a common activity in which almost all people engage. It is probably the most universal of human experiences. As Henry Ford, inventor of the Model T, said, "There will never be a system invented which will do away with the necessity of work." For many people, work takes up most of their day. They spend more time with their coworkers than with family and friends. And the common goals people pursue on the job may be among the first thoughts that they have in the morning, and the last that they may have at night.

While the idea of work is universal, the way it is done and who performs it vary considerably throughout history. The story of work is inextricably tied to the history of technology, the history of culture, and the history of gender and race. When the typewriter was invented, for example, it was considered the exclusive domain of men who worked as secretaries. As women workers became more accepted, the secretarial role was gradually filled by women. Finally, with the invention of the computer, the modern secretary spends little time actually typing correspondence. Files are delivered via computer, and more time is spent on other tasks than the manual typing of correspondence and business.

This is just one example of how work brings together technology, gender, and culture. Another example is the American plantation slave. The harvesting of cotton was initially so cumbersome and time consuming that even with slaves its profitability was doubtful. With the invention of the cotton gin, however, efficiency improved, and slavery became a viable agricultural tool. It also became a southern tradition and institution, enough that the South was willing to go to war to preserve it.

The books in Lucent's Working Life series strive to show the intermingling of work, and its reflection in culture, technology, race, and gender. Indeed, history viewed through the perspective of the average worker is both enlightening and fascinating. Take the history of the typewriter, mentioned above. Readers today have access to more technology than any of their historical counterparts, and, in fact, though they would find the typewriter's keyboard familiar, they would find using it a bore. Finding out that people spent their days sitting over that machine (with no talk of carpal tunnel syndrome!) and were valued if they made no typing errors because corrections were cumbersome to make and, in some legal professions, made documents invalid, is an interesting story that involves many different aspects of history.

The desire to work is almost innate. As German socialist Ferdinand Lassalle said in the 1850s, "Workingmen we all are so far as we have the desire to make ourselves useful to human society in any way whatever." Yet each historical period offers a million different stories of the history of each job and how it was performed. And that history is the history of human society.

Each book in the Working Life series strives to tell the tale of these anonymous workers. Primary source quotes offer veracity and immediacy to each volume, letting the workers themselves tell their stories. In addition, thorough bibliographies tell students where they can find out more information, and complete indexes allow for easy perusal of the text. While students learn about the work of years gone by, they gain empathy for those who toil and, perhaps, a universal pride in taking up the work that will someday be theirs.

WHO WERE THE KNIGHTS?

Few historical periods have captured the imagination of the public more than the Middle Ages, a period of European history beginning with the crumbling of the Roman Empire in A.D. 500 and the flowering of the Renaissance in 1300. Few images from that period are more emblematic of the times than the "noble knight." The mere mention of the words triggers romanticized notions of medieval knights displaying the chivalric qualities of loyalty, honor, courtesy, and courage. They also conjure images of knights defending their hilltop castles, charging in full armor astride mighty warhorses, and in times of peace, riding throughout villages dispensing justice, directing yeoman farmers in their hay fields, assisting people in need, and attending to a variety of other knightly responsibilities.

All of these images combine to create the modern archetypal traits of the "knight in shining armor." They define the working life of a medieval knight, first and foremost, as a warrior preparing, equipping, and training for battle. Second, the images define the working life of the knight during times of peace when he exchanged his armor for riding clothes and assumed a different set of responsibilities as a civic leader.

But to what degree is this present image of the medieval knight a fair and accurate portrait of his working life? Over the years, even some respected historians have succumbed to a romantic view of the knight where fantasy sometimes overwhelms reality. However, medieval documents and publications by respected contemporary historians present more accurate insights into the working life of a medieval knight. And to gain a better understanding of a knight's working life it is necessary to look back at the place and time of their origin.

THE ORIGINS OF THE KNIGHT

Knights did not exist in Europe before the Middle Ages. A series of historical events following the decline of Rome conspired to create a unique job that disappeared with the approach of the Renaissance.

After the Roman Empire crumbled and Europeans were no longer protected by Roman legions, a stable economy, and law, they suffered a series of invasions by Germanic and Middle Eastern warriors who swept across Europe. These warriors fought with incomparable skill on horseback. To respond to this threat, local men began developing their own equestrian skills, and the job of the knight was born. A line of charging knights on horseback with lances in hand could easily crush opposing foot soldiers and effectively counter other mounted warriors.

By the eighth century, knights began to emerge as the most important warriors on the battlefield. One century later, in 806, Charlemagne, king of the Franks (early French), scripted the earliest known and most significant letter articulating the unique relationship between knights and their nobles, laying the basis for the working life of knights:

You shall come with your men prepared to go on warlike service to any part of our realm that we may point out; that is, you shall come with arms and gear and all warlike equipment of clothing and food. Every horseman shall have

More than just a romantic ideal, the medieval knight was a warrior on horseback and village protector.

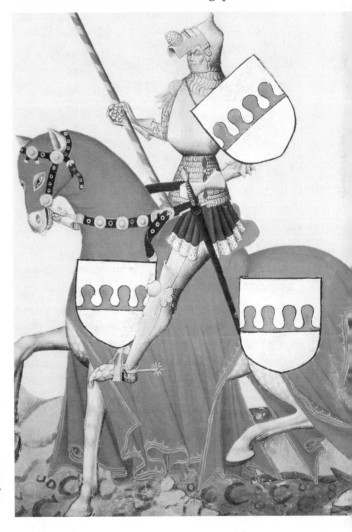

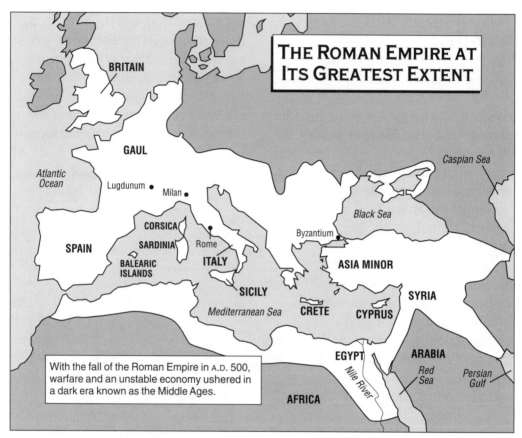

THE ROMAN EMPIRE AT ITS GREATEST EXTENT

BRITAIN

GAUL

Atlantic Ocean

Lugdunum • Milan •

Caspian Sea

CORSICA

SARDINIA   Rome

SPAIN

BALEARIC ISLANDS

ITALY

Byzantium

Black Sea

ASIA MINOR

SICILY

Mediterranean Sea   CRETE   CYPRUS

SYRIA

EGYPT   ARABIA

With the fall of the Roman Empire in A.D. 500, warfare and an unstable economy ushered in a dark era known as the Middle Ages.

Nile River

Red Sea

Persian Gulf

AFRICA

shield, lance, sword, a dagger, a bow and a quiver. Upon your carts you shall have ready spades, axes, picks, and iron-pointed stakes, and all other things needed for battle. The rations shall be for three months, the clothing must last for six.[1]

THE KNIGHT'S SOCIAL POSITION

Though their social status varied throughout Europe, early knights had little money and were mostly free peasants rather than wealthy noblemen. By the early tenth century, however, as the knights' skills on the battlefield increased, their value to kings and nobles increased their social status. Knights gradually merged into the lower echelon of the aristocracy and within a century they became synonymous with the nobility. Sons born to nobility came to bear the title of knight when they reached maturity; noblemen and knights were virtually one and the same.

At this time, the social structure of Europe had three distinct social strata, represented by the shape of a pyramid.

At the apex stood a handful of nobles and knights representing about 1 percent of the population. Below them was another small stratum of another 1 or 2 percent representing the Catholic clergy. At the base, which was extremely broad, was the remaining vast majority of poor peasant farmers and simple shop owners toiling to support the other two classes.

European rulers, especially kings and powerful lords, depended on knights to protect their territories, yet needed a way to pay for their warring services. In an economy with little hard currency such as gold and silver coins, land was the answer. In return for a parcel of farmland and a village or two from the king or a noble, a knight agreed to fight for his benefactor and to administrate and protect the land. The knight in turn handed the land over to peasant farmers and craftspeople for their use in return for annual payments of goods and services to equip a knight with horse and armor—both very expensive commodities. In this simple system, land was at the heart of the economy and each person existing within it had informal yet clearly defined obligations.

Without a law code or law enforcement officers, however, some armed knights, especially those with little money, took advantage of their power and committed crimes against unarmed citizens with impunity. While roaming the countryside some armed knights robbed travelers, stole food from farmers and innkeepers and burglarized homes. Hoping to rein in their aggressive behavior, the Catholic Church acted to place controls over them.

CHIVALRY AND THE CHURCH

In 989, at a time when rule of law meant rule of the sword, uneducated, self-serving, armed knights often ran amock. Worried that their violence to unarmed peasants and clergy members was threatening the church's role in society as well as its property, the pope in Rome made a move to rein in reckless knights by obligating them to the church. The resulting Peace of God edict threatened sanctions against any knight who raided churches, attacked unarmed clergy, or robbed peasants or those traveling to or from church. The Peace of God edict required strengthening in 1063 by the Truce of God, which ordered knights to forgo war between Thursday and Sunday and on all holy days as well as on days commemorating saints. With these two edicts, knights were forced by threat of papal condemnation to accept the role of protector of the poor and the church.

Contained within these two edicts were the seeds of chivalry, a code of behavior aimed at controlling knights' bellicose behavior. It was the opinion of church leaders that in addition to fighting for the nobility, knights had the additional ethical and moral obligation to help unarmed citizens in need of assistance. Chivalry was based on courtesy and honor toward the church as well as the innocent and defenseless poor. Once medieval society had defined the knights' social position, source of income, and chivalric obligations, their job description snapped into focus. A twelfth-century philosopher, John of Salisbury, posed the question, "What is the function of orderly knighthood?" His answer, which reflected a knight's chivalric obligations, was respected and repeated by many knights who revered him:

To defend the Church, to assail infidelity, to venerate the priesthood, to protect the poor from injuries, to pacify

A knight leads peasants to safety as his besieged castle falls. Protecting his villagers was one of the knight's chief duties.

the province, to pour out their blood for their brothers, and, if need be, to lay down their lives. The high praises of God are in their throat, and two-edged swords are in their hands to execute punishment on the nations and rebuke upon the peoples, and to bind their kings and their nobles in links of iron."[2]

Achieving knighthood was not an easy task. Learning how to defend the church, protect the poor, and wield the two-edged sword took years of training and dedication. Before medieval society would recognize a noble youngster as a knight, he needed to complete an apprenticeship, which defined and consumed most of his childhood.

CHAPTER 1

THE APPRENTICESHIP OF A KNIGHT

The journey to knighthood began at birth. In nearly all cases, noble birth was a prerequisite for all boys destined to take the title of knight. Because youthful strength and agility were two of the principal qualities of a successful knight, boys began training at an early age so they were ready for the battlefield in the prime of their life. Knights were in their fighting prime during their twenties and thirties, and as they approached forty most who had survived the bloody battlefields were expected to retire to their manors and focus on civic administration. Older knights oversaw fields and livestock, small village businesses, and local justice, and sired the next generation of knights.

THE FORGING OF A KNIGHT

No military schools existed in medieval Europe to train and forge knights. They received their training and education, as was the case with virtually all other occupations, through apprenticeship. This system of training stressed learning by following the example of an experienced knight acting as a mentor.

The apprenticeship of a knight occupied boys during most of their youth. Beginning at an age somewhere between five and seven, and continuing for at least ten years and sometimes fifteen years, nearly all boys born into the nobility were expected to learn how to defend their homelands in times of war and to administer it in times of peace. One medieval manuscript referring to the apprenticeship of a knight noted three seven-year periods of training:

Page at 7, squire at 14, a lad bent on knighthood trained for combat man-to-man. He learned to struggle swinging the fearsome flail, dodge the battle-ax that could cleave his helm [helmet], and wield the sword—also to swear oaths on holy relics on his knob [the hilt end of a sword]. Knighted at 21, he donned his spurs and rode to glory.[3]

What made the forging of a knight particularly unusual was that it was not performed by the boy's parents. The common thinking of the time was that another home would provide a more disciplined environment that the young lad would take more seriously. The basic rule in England and parts of France was that the lord overseeing multiple villages was responsible for the apprenticeship of his knights' sons. In 1216, England's King Henry III made the lord's duty law by decreeing, "The lord hath the right to the nurture of the vassal's child."[4] The law provided the lord with two advantages: First it ensured that the young knights growing

After years of living with another family during his apprenticeship, a young man returns home as a knight.

a lord with a large number of knights to spend a great deal of his resources training, clothing, and feeding the boys. To provide relief, tradition gradually changed to allow other noble families to assist in the apprenticeships. This meant that parents could choose the most suitable home for their sons.

When parents believed their son was ready to begin the long and arduous road to knighthood, they sought another noble family to assume the responsibilities of preparing him. The choice of households was a solemn one. Parents understood that although their boy would return home during his apprenticeship for holidays, birthdays, and occasional holy events, most of his time growing into manhood would be spent under the tutelage of another family. Parents always looked for a family of equal or greater wealth, authority, and social prestige for the sake of their son and for their own social standing as well. They further understood that once their son was out the door, they too could expect to be asked to perform the same obligation by another family.

Refusal to accept a boy was rare because parents always made discreet inquiries before formally asking the fa-

up under his watchful eye would be loyal to him once knighthood was conferred, and second, the young men would receive the best training from the ablest instructors the lord could find.

The arrangement, however, had one major drawback. It proved difficult for

vor. On those rare occasions when a request was met by a refusal, relationships between those two families might be strained for many generations and could later determine which side each took in a local dispute.

THE PAGE

During the first seven years of his apprenticeship, the boy was called a page, a generic term used for anyone performing menial duties in a household or shop. The only difference between a page during his apprenticeship and other pages was the recognition that the former would advance to knighthood.

Within the home of his new parents, the page initially remained close to the lady of the house and her lady servants for motherly care and training. They instructed him in the expected behavior of a knight, which included general courtesies toward his elders, understanding biblical ideas, cleanliness, proper manners, dancing, music appreciation, and even how to slice meat correctly. In most cases, reading and writing were not taught, however, because formal academic pursuits during the Middle Ages were generally left to the clergy.

A page also had to perform physical chores in the castle as well as out-of-doors. Indoor obligations included setting the table, lighting candles, serving meals, cleaning dishes, chopping wood, and lighting fires to warm bedrooms. Out-of-doors, pages worked in the garden planting and tending rows of vegetables, drawing water from the well or nearby stream, and chasing chickens for dinner, then chopping off their heads, soaking them in hot water, and plucking them.

Once pages reached adolescence, they rose to the higher status of squires, a term borrowed from the French word *écuyer*, meaning shield bearer. No longer under the direction of the women of the house, they were expected to begin to train for warfare with the men. Following a brief rite-of-passage ceremony attended by their parents, pages received a simple sword symbolizing their passage into a more mature position.

THE SQUIRE

At fourteen, the taller, stronger, and more self-confident squire departed the castle to become the personal attendant to a selected knight. A contemporary medieval historian describes the squire's job this way:

A squire was first and foremost the personal servant of a knight. Secondly he was a knight in training. The term servant has negative connotations today that were not there in medieval times. A servant was "one who serves" and it was a high honor to serve in fealty as a squire to a knight. In the Middle Ages the relationship under the oath of fealty took precedence over and often took the place of one's family.[5]

✦ ENDURING THE WEIGHT OF ARMOR ✦

One of the more critical tasks that all squires had to accomplish before becoming a knight was to build enough muscle to fight under the weight of a suit of armor. This included the strength needed to mount a horse unassisted. This maneuver was crucial to survival on the battlefield in the event that a knight might be unhorsed and without his squire to help him back on. One revealing medieval French description of a squire working to gain strength and endurance for armed battle is from "The Structure of Medieval Society" at the Sara Douglass Web site, www.saradouglass.com.

Now cased in armour, he would practice leaping on to the back of a horse; alone, to accustom himself to become long-winded. And enduring, he would walk and run long distances on foot, or he would practice striking numerous and forcible blows with a battle-axe. . . . In order to accustom himself to the weight of his armour, he would turn somersaults while clad in a complete suit of mail, with the exception of his helmet, or would dance vigorously in a shirt of steel. He would place one hand on the saddle-bow of a tall charger, and the other on his [the horse's] neck, and he would vault over him. . . . He would climb up between two walls that stood four or five feet [apart] by the mere [strength] of his arms and legs, and would thus reach the top, even if it were a tower, without resting in either ascent or descent. . . . When he was at home, he would practice with the other young esquires at lance-throwing and other warlike exercises, and this continually in armour.

Physical development was essential for a squire. Each had to gain the weight and strength necessary to fight in armor that could weigh sixty pounds or more—close to half the weight of the average young knight who stood just five and a half feet tall. In addition, squires needed to develop the muscle to wear armor for several hours during battle while also wielding a heavy iron sword or battle-ax. One way a squire gained muscle was by wearing baggy clothing with dirt sewn into pockets, hems, and collars to weigh them down.

Once muscle was added, the young man focused his attention on practicing his martial skills and horsemanship until he mastered both. According to medieval texts and drawings, young squires learned to handle weapons first on foot and without armor. They practiced running and hitting targets with a lance or engaged in mock combat exercises with wooden swords that were not lethal but could leave painful welts on those who failed to parry attacks. Later, the squires learned to master the same skills in full armor with iron swords, and finally while riding a horse.

A squire was also an attendant to his mentor. He served his master at the dinner table, looked after his master's horses, polished his weapons and armor, and when preparing his master for a battle or a tournament, assisted him into his armor and onto his horse. As the squire grew older, he was expected to follow his master into battle, protect his master if he fell in battle, provide first aid if needed, and bring back the knight's body if he was killed in battle.

To prepare the squire for his civic and social responsibilities when not at war, squires accompanied knights on hunting rides that sent their mounts crashing through dense forests, vaulting stone walls, and splashing across streams in pursuit of deer and wild boar. They also accompanied knights as they made their village rounds. They learned how to oversee farmers and tradesmen and how to administer justice if laws were violated.

Squires mastered military skills and horsemanship by engaging in mock battles, which prepared them for real combat.

HONOR AND THE CODE OF CHIVALRY

The apprenticeship of a knight, in addition to training for war and civic administration, included indoctrination into a code of moral behavior known as chivalry. Civic and religious leaders understood that knights were the dominant armed faction in medieval society and as such, wielded the awesome power to perform both good and evil acts. To encourage the best behavior possible both on and off the battlefield, an elaborate code of ethics evolved over many generations. These ethics encouraged respectful behavior toward others and discouraged selfish, reckless acts. In this regard, the code of chivalry was a set of rules to limit senseless bloodshed by placing social controls over heavily armed and potentially dangerous men.

The term chivalry, derived from the French word for horse, *cheval*, indicates that chivalric behavior was intended for those who rode horses—the knights. Chivalry was in full bloom by the eleventh century, when manuals were published throughout Europe outlining rules of honorable conduct. The rules governing battlefield behavior emphasized fair play, such as never killing a defenseless adversary whose sword has been broken and sparing the life of

ᴥ A SQUIRE'S UNUSUAL TRAINING ᴥ

During a squire's training he was required to pay attention to his knight's preparations and needs for battle. Suiting him up in his armor, saddling his horse, and assisting him if he was unhorsed on the battlefield were responsibilities for all squires. Some requirements, however, may have caused squires to wonder about the purpose of their apprenticeship.

A small book published in the twelfth century titled The Book of Nature *outlined many of the responsibilities of a loyal squire. It also included a description of the squire's nightly mundane responsibilities readying his knight for bed. This account is from Walter Clifford Meller's* A Knight's Life in the Days of Chivalry.

When he (the knight) has supped and goes to his chamber, take off his gown, and lay it up in such place as ye best know. Put a mantle on his back to keep his body from cold, pull off his shoes, socks, and hose, and throw these over your shoulder. Comb his hair, but first kneel down and put his kerchief and nightcap around and over him in a seemly fashion. Have the bed, sheet, and pillow ready for him and when he is in bed draw the curtains round about it and see that there is enough nite-lite [fire] to last the night. Then, drive out the dog and the cat, giving them a clout and take leave of your lord, bow low to him and retire.

a fallen knight by offering him an opportunity to surrender. Yet, chivalry also encouraged knights to fight on for the sake of their personal honor even when bloodied and beaten.

Rules governing conduct off the battlefield also stressed honorable behavior. It was this aspect of chivalry that interested church leaders because there were no laws or law enforcement officers to control the behavior of armed men. The chivalric code instilled by the church required knights to protect and defend the rights of the poor and the weak, especially women and children. Each knight was expected to be honest in all public dealings, to never steal, to respect the rights of others, and to act humbly toward the poor and clerics. Each also swore to defend his lord, king, homeland, and the Christian church. A twelfth-century French writer, Chrétien de Troyes, provided this definition of chivalry that he condensed from several code manuals:

> A knight must be merciful without wickedness, affable without treachery, compassionate towards the suffering, and open handed. He must be ready to help the needy and to confound robbers and murderers, a just judge without favor or hate. He must prefer death to dishonor. He must protect the Holy Church for she cannot defend herself.[6]

ACHIEVING KNIGHTHOOD

Knighthood was not achieved until each squire was evaluated and deemed ready to carry on the long traditions and responsibilities befitting a knight. Honoring the code of chivalry was important, as was learning good manners and how to justly administer an estate, but no responsibility outweighed the importance of a knight's demonstrating his military skills against his peers at tournaments. These tournaments were mock battles fought between small armies or individual combatants, and were sometimes as brutal and deadly as real warfare. This component of knighthood tested a knight's commitment more than anything else. Roger de Hoveden, an English chronicler living in the mid–twelfth century, revealed the singular importance of learning combat skills in tournaments:

> A squire cannot shine in war if he has not prepared for it in tournaments. He must have seen his own blood flow, have had his teeth crackle under the blow of his adversary, and have been dashed to earth with such force as to feel the weight of his foe, and disarmed twenty times; he must twenty times retrieve his failures. Then will he be able to confront actual battle with the hope of being victorious."[7]

When all requirements were generally fulfilled to his mentor's satisfaction

After being ceremonially recognized as a gentleman and a member of the warrior class, a knight bows to his king.

or the young man reached the age of twenty-one and was needed to fight wars, his mentor notified the squire's father to prepare for his son's knighting ceremony.

THE KNIGHTING CEREMONY

Initially, during the ninth and tenth centuries, the knighting ceremony was little more than an open-hand, bone-jarring blow to the neck, followed by an admonition by a squire's knight to conduct himself with bravery and honor. By the eleventh century, the ceremony of knighthood had become more civilized. It was filled with pretentious ceremony symbolizing the importance of a knight's authority, the attainment of a young gentleman's manhood, and his entrance into the warrior class of the social elite. Such ceremonies were costly for the young man's father.

The full ceremony lasted several days and was filled with symbolic meaning. It began at the church with a nightlong prayer vigil. During the vigil the young man's weapons were placed on the altar, symbolizing the role of the church in the future life of the knight. This was followed by a sunrise bath, representing the washing away of youthful in-discretion so that he would be prepared for a man's duty in bloody battle. After the bath, he dressed in a simple white linen tunic symbolizing purity, a scarlet mantle for nobility, and black shoes denoting his eventual death. A priest then said Mass for him before a gathering of royal friends and family. Breakfast was then served for the entire assembly, which was followed by a processional walk to the great hall in

---

GEOFFREY OF ANJOU BECOMES A KNIGHT

The knighting ceremony was always a splendid moment for the new knight and his family. Some ceremonies were far more extravagant than others, depending upon the social rank of the knight's family. Historians Frances and Joseph Gies provide this description of one of the most elaborate knighting ceremonies for a French knight named Geoffrey of Anjou, in their book Daily Life in Medieval Times.

When Geoffrey entered the inner chamber of the King's Hall surrounded by knights, the King went to meet him, affectionately embracing and kissing him, and taking him by the hand to a seat for a day of joyful celebration. At the first dawn of the next day, a bath was prepared, according to the custom for novice knights. After bathing, Geoffrey donned a linen undergarment, a tunic of cloth of gold, a purple robe, silk stockings, and shoes ornamented with golden lions. He then left the chamber to appear in public. Horses and arms were brought and distributed. A Spanish horse of wonderful beauty was provided for Geoffrey, swifter than the flight of birds. He was then armed with double-woven mail, which no lance or javelin could pierce, and shod with iron boots; golden spurs; a shield with golden lions was hung around his neck, a helmet was placed on his head gleaming with many precious stones, and which no sword could pierce or mar; a spear of ash tipped with iron was provided; and finally an ancient sword. Thus our novice knight was armed, the future flower of knighthood, who despite his armor leapt with marvelous agility on his horse. For seven days the celebration in honor of the new knight continued.

the castle, where ornate clothes made of silks and satins were given to the young man.

Before family and friends, the candidate for knighthood donned his armor complete with his spurs—the small metal barbs attached to the heel of a rider's boot and used to control a horse's movements—in a brief ceremony called "winning his spurs." Next, the young man's mentor gave him his most important and symbolic weapon, his sword. The act of fastening the sword of knighthood upon him, called the *cingulum militiae*, created a bond between the lord and the new knight.

Kneeling before the lord conducting the ceremony, the squire repeated a brief oath promising to fight for and protect the general welfare of all common citizens, and solemnly bowed his head. At that moment, the lord stepped forward and drew his own sword, holding it high above the young man's head. Calling out the squire's name, the lord then conferred knighthood by placing the flat side of his sword blade on one shoulder of the squire's and then the other. These two symbolic blows, called the *collée* in France and the *dubbing* in England, marked the moment the squire became a knight.

This elaborate ceremony was the standard for most young squires. On occasion, a squire who followed his mentor into battle found himself engaged in combat, for which he was re- warded and honored with his dubbing ceremony on the battlefield.

BATTLEFIELD DUBBING

Conferring knighthood on a squire immediately after the savagery of a battle while the smell of blood was still in the air was considered the most glorious circumstance for this solemn ceremony. Under such circumstances, knighthood could be bestowed in two distinctly different ways. The more common of the two was for a nobleman or even a king to confer knighthood on one or several squires who had fought valiantly during a successful battle. At the end of the day, while dead bodies still littered the battlefield, the victorious leader would dub each worthy squire with his sword while the rest of the army witnessed the ceremony.

The more unusual knighting ceremony occurred when a vanquished knight who was badly wounded wished to surrender. The rules of chivalry permitted a knight to surrender only to another knight, yet on rare occasions, a squire was the victorious warrior. Under such rare circumstances, a knight taken prisoner, even though he was an enemy, was compelled to perform the dubbing ceremony on his victor before he could properly surrender his sword. The dialog of such an unusual ceremony is recorded by historian Walter Meller in his book *A Knight's Life in the Days of Chivalry*. A beaten English knight asked his victorious French opponent before surrendering his sword, "Are you a knight and a gentleman?" "I am a gentleman," the Frenchman replied, "but I am not yet a knight."[8] At that moment, the Englishman requested that he kneel, dubbed him, and then surrendered his sword to the novice knight.

Once knighthood was conferred, the novice knight faced the mundane reality of properly equipping himself for his future profession. To do so, a considerable amount of money was required before riding off to war or taking charge of his estate.

CHAPTER 2

EQUIPPING A KNIGHT

The profession of knighthood required a knight to acquire an extensive and expensive array of equipment to perform both his military and civic responsibilities. In the role of the warrior, each knight was responsible for acquiring weaponry.

By the eleventh century, knights went on military campaigns protected by a suit of mail, body armor, shield, lance, and sword. They were attended by one or more assistants and brought an assortment of horses. In the role of defender of his village, each knight was responsible for providing his house, preferably a stone castle, as a place of refuge to which all villagers could flee in times of invasion.

CHAIN MAIL

The earliest knights learned that they could enhance their odds of surviving vicious sword attacks by covering their bodies with some form of protective ar-

mor. The earliest form of body armor was chain mail, more commonly referred to as mail. Made from thousands of interconnected hard metal rings, it was woven into a flexible outer garment that offered protection against slicing sword blows. Its origins stretch back to the late Roman Empire, but its first widespread use was found in the early Middle Ages.

Required for every knight was the hauberk, a shirt of mail extending from the shoulders to the knees. The hauberk of Charlemagne's day during the early ninth century was pulled on over the head. It had short sleeves and a plain round neck opening starting just above the shoulders. At the center front and back it was split from hem to groin to enable the wearer to straddle his mount. Beneath the hauberk, knights wore a quilted or padded jacket called a *gambeson* to prevent chafing and lacerations of the skin. The standard hauberk weighed about twenty pounds, but on

A Knight's Armor

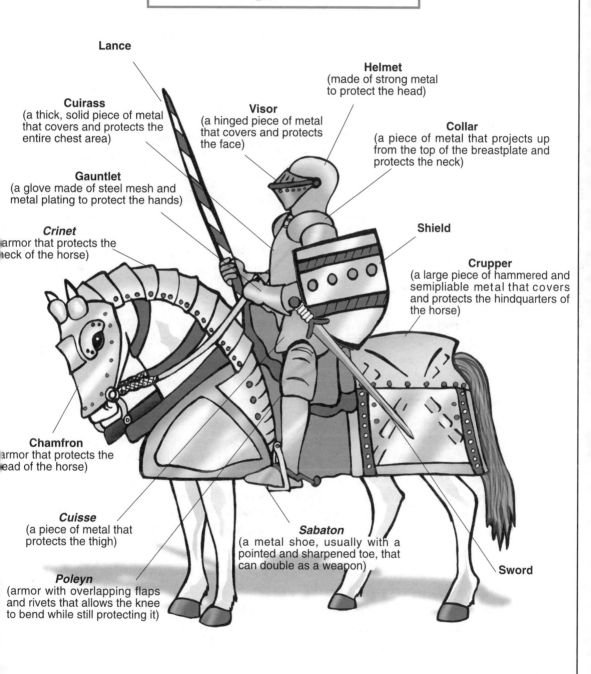

Lance

Cuirass
(a thick, solid piece of metal
that covers and protects the
entire chest area)

Visor
(a hinged piece of metal
that covers and protects
the face)

Helmet
(made of strong metal
to protect the head)

Collar
(a piece of metal that projects up
from the top of the breastplate and
protects the neck)

Gauntlet
(a glove made of steel mesh and
metal plating to protect the hands)

Crinet
armor that protects the
neck of the horse)

Shield

Crupper
(a large piece of hammered and
semipliable metal that covers
and protects the hindquarters of
the horse)

Chamfron
armor that protects the
ead of the horse)

Cuisse
(a piece of metal that
protects the thigh)

Sabaton
(a metal shoe, usually with a
pointed and sharpened toe, that
can double as a weapon)

Sword

Poleyn
(armor with overlapping flaps
and rivets that allows the knee
to bend while still protecting it)

◈ FABRICATING CHAIN MAIL ◈

Creating chain mail was a long, laborious, and expensive process. But for the knights who could afford it, mail was essential because of its strength and ability to be shaped into virtually any form and worn like a garment.

The construction of mail began by hammering a sheet of metal very thin and flat.

The sheet was then cut into narrow strips, and each strip wound around an iron rod. The wound wire or strips were sliced along the rod, and the result of each cutting was a handful of open rings.

The fabricator looped each link inside another and then riveted each link closed to join them together. This was done by first flattening the open ends of the ring, punching a hole in each flattened end, and inserting a rivet through both holes. Mail could be strengthened by including in the design a series of rings that had been punched from a sheet of metal instead of having been wound, cut, and then riveted. Punched links had no weak spot where the rivet was driven, and the use of them in the mail made the armor less likely to be breached.

To make a suit of chain mail, a blacksmith joined one ring to four or six others and joined each of these to another four or six links, and so on, until he had "woven" his metal fabric to the desired size. The number of rings used in each linking varied, depending on how the worker wished to shape his garment. Mail that linked each ring to six others was much denser than mail that used only four. For particularly effective armor, two links were used for every link used in ordinary mail; the result was called double mail and it weighed twice as much.

occasion, when a knight had extra money, he might purchase a double hauberk that weighed twice as much but offered twice the protection.

To provide similar protection to the head and neck, the knight wore a coif, a chain mail hood worn over the head and under the helmet while leaving the face exposed. Mail coverings were made for virtually every part of the body, and in addition to hauberks and coifs, knights often used leggings, foot coverings, and even mail gloves.

The foremost advantage of mail was its defense against bladed weapons; a sword, no matter how sharp, could not easily slash through the metal links. But mail also had disadvantages. If a knight was forced to flee on foot, throwing off the hauberk was incredibly difficult. In fact, knights practiced their extrication from it to increase their chances for survival. In addition, sometimes a warrior was wounded but was unaware of the seriousness of the wound because the chain mail disguised it. Such was the case of the knight King Olaf Trygva-son from Norway whose personal historian recorded an instance in the midst of a battle: "As he stretched down his right hand, some observed that blood was running down under his steel glove, but no one knew where he was wounded."[9]

Mail, however, did not make its wearer invulnerable; the force of the blow from a club or mace (a club with a spiked iron ball at one end) could crush the flesh and bones beneath the mail. Besides, as time passed, weapons, such as bows and arrows and crossbows, evolved to penetrate it. Arrows shot by archers with bows at close range could break through mail. The iron-tipped arrows shot from the crossbow could travel up to a quarter of a mile and penetrate a knight's mail effortlessly. To protect themselves more effectively, knights began to wear suits of heavy plate armor they named "harnesses."

PLATE ARMOR

Archaeologists working with historians conclude that plate armor began to be used around the second half of the thirteenth century. The advantage of plate armor over chain mail was that its solid sheets of iron resisted direct hits by arrows, lances, or spear points while also effectively deflecting their grazing blows.

Early plate armor was first used to cover the shins, forearms, and chest. It was custom-made to fit a man's di-mensions. However, early plate was less than reliable because it was handmade by blacksmiths who often failed to create thick enough plate. For this reason, early plate was not completely trusted and was worn over chain mail. Over time, however, higher-quality plate removed the need for mail.

The difficulty of designing the plate armor was that it needed to be flexible enough to move while covering jointed parts of the body such as knees, elbows, ankles, wrists, and knuckles. To protect these vulnerable body parts, at first small pieces of plate were sewn together with heavy thread. These were then laced together through holes drilled into the edges of the plates. Such loosely stitched armor increased protection and mobility but left gaps between the plates that exposed too much soft tissue.

The solution to this problem came during the latter part of the fourteenth century when the first true body armor known as a brigandine was developed. This armor utilized small overlapping plates, held together with small leather straps and gliding rivets, which slid over each other as they moved to give greater flexibility as body joints moved. These plates were also held in place by rivets attached to a canvas garment that was worn under the armor. This was usually covered in some finer material such as silk to avoid chafing the skin.

The brigandine was an exceptional artistic and engineering creation. It

Chain mail (left) offered limited protection during battle. Only plate armor (right) was able to resist direct hits from arrows, lances, and spears.

even provided effective coverage for individual fingers and sufficient mobility to allow the knight to grip his weapons. The complexity and effectiveness of the brigandine are revealed by the more than two hundred individual pieces of plate used in a single suit.

Knights of the late Middle Ages were well protected but at the expense of mobility. Complete suits weighing between sixty and sometimes seventy pounds were effective while mounted but a liability when the knight was unhorsed. Although an unhorsed knight could still recover to fight on foot, his quickness was no match for a foot soldier in mail or no armor at all. Horrific stories pepper medieval texts describing the hideous deaths of armored knights incapable of escaping from their armored caskets.

Some were rolled into rivers and drowned, while others were trapped by impromptu bonfires built around them and burned to death inside their armor. Still others were knocked off their feet and sat upon by attackers who slid daggers between overlapping plates where soft tissue was vulnerable, and through eye slits in their helmets, causing the knight to die a slow and painful death.

Suits of armor from the late Middle Ages like these offered knights full-body protection, but they hampered their mobility.

The Helmet

The quintessential component of the knight's armor was his helmet. Archaeologists have discovered them in a greater variety of styles than any other piece of a knight's equipment. The style chosen was based on the leading edge technology of the time as well as personal artistic taste.

Regardless of the century, the helmet was made from a single piece of plate, with the sole exception of those with a face visor that could be raised and lowered for eating and drinking. The early helmets of the tenth and eleventh centuries were conical in shape. The twelfth century opened with knights wearing the barrel helmet. Its distinctive design was its flat top and movable visor that covered the entire face except for two slits for the eyes and breathing holes at the mouth.

Helmet designs, however, had flaws. The barrel helmet was susceptible to hard sword blows because the top was flat and did not deflect the blows. Instead the impact of the blow was absorbed right into the knight's skull. Archaeologists have uncovered the split-open skulls of slain knights still inside these bucket-shaped helmets, evidence of instant death by a sword blow.

The solution to the barrel helmet's defect was a design called the *bascinet*. This design introduced the rounded top with the addition of a crest, a raised solid ridge running from the front to the back. Both improvements helped deflect the impact of a hard blow in such a way as to prevent the sword edge from cutting through the helmet. For example, in one story, following a particularly fierce battle, a squire was sent to locate his knight who had mysteriously disappeared from the battlefield. Having desperately searched everywhere, the squire finally made some inquiries at a nearby village about his mentor and was directed to the blacksmith's shop. Approaching it, the squire spied his master bent over with his head still in his helmet, resting on an anvil. His helmet had received so many blows during the battle that the blacksmith had to hammer it back into shape before it could be removed from the knight's head.

The Shield

A helmet and body armor alone were not sufficient to protect the knight effectively. To fend off initial sword, lance, and arrow attacks, each knight carried a shield as his first-line weapon of defense. Its early round design, handed down from the Greeks and Romans, gradually gave way to a rectangular shape rounded at the top and slightly pointed at the bottom nicknamed the kite. The kite provided more effective coverage of the body.

The mounted knight always carried his shield with his left arm, with the rounded end at the top. This protected him from neck to ankle. To avoid tiring

ᐧᓸ **SUITING UP CAP-A-PIE** ᐧᓹ

Suiting up a knight cap-a-pie, a French term meaning "head to foot," required the assistance of a knight's squire. Slipping into mail was easy enough, but a full suit of plate armor required thirty minutes to lace and buckle.

For the sake of comfort, the first layer of dressing a knight wore was undergarments made of canvas and soft silk. These covered the knight's entire skin to prevent chafing and excessive perspiration. Once clothed, the squire worked from the feet up. The heavy articulated armor-plated shoes called *sabatons* were secured by lacing the leather boots through holes in the plate. Leather straps and metal buckles secured the *sabatons* to the heel. Next the squire attached hinged *grieves* over the calves and shins by clamping front and back together and buckling the *poleyn,* the section protecting the knees, in two places behind the knee. The thigh area,

just above the knee, was then covered by a two-piece *cuisse* that clamped and buckled together.

The section of plate armor covering the chest, back, and waist was the cuirass. Made in two large sections, one for the front and the other for the back, the squire secured the two sections over the knight's shoulders with buckles. Once squared up and properly balanced, the knight called for the upper arm and lower arm sections, and finally the gloves called gauntlets. The plates of these complicated sections were permanently riveted to leather gloves to guarantee a quick and secure fit.

The final touch included placing the helmet on the knight, which rested on his shoulder armor, followed by spurs and the knight's sword belt. During the entire process, the knight would flex his arms, rotate his waist, and bend at the knees to secure a proper fit.

his arm on long rides, the shield was slung over his neck or shoulder by a leather strap. When the call to get into battle formation was sounded on the trumpet, however, the knight would slide his forearm through a shorter strap on the inside of the shield and grab a wood pommel—a handgrip attached to the shield—that allowed for quick manipulation.

Maneuverability was a key consideration for shield design and composi-

tion. To maintain as light a design as possible yet one that still provided strength, shields were made of several thin layers of wood—each laid with the grain running in opposite directions. These were then glued and nailed together. The wood was covered in ox hide, which was made exceptionally hard by boiling it in water first. This combination of materials and design provided strength yet lightness for quick one-armed maneuverability.

By the fourteenth century, knights had retired their shields. No longer needed with the advent of good-quality plate armor, shields were discontinued in favor of better offensive weapons. The key offensive weapons were the lance and the sword.

THE LANCE AND SWORD

The lance, which was used exclusively by knights fighting on horseback, was between eight and twelve feet long and two inches thick. It was made of a hard, durable wood such as ash, poplar, or cedar. The pointed end was capped with a sharp metal tip.

The lance was carried to a battlefield by the knight's squire and then handed to the knight moments before the charge. Initially the knight held the lance in a vertical position resting the butt end in his right stirrup. But when the charge commenced, the knight shifted the lance by cradling it under his right arm pit and holding it tightly with the right hand and arm against his side. The knight then aimed it at an onrushing opponent. The objective was to use the momentum of horse and rider to drive the point of the lance through the enemy's armor. Because the lance was difficult to maneuver, the knight had only one opportunity to hit his opponent before he abandoned the long lance in favor of a shorter sword to be used in close combat.

The sword was the most lethal weapon on the battlefield. While arrows and other projectiles were commonly used in combat by foot soldiers, most fighting and killing among knights was done with the sword. Swords were expensive items, and so they were highly prized. They were often passed down from father to son for many generations. Some were given heroic names, while others were inscribed with the names of great battles or notched and used as primitive counters of those who were killed by its blade.

Swords were made of the hardest steel or iron available because they had to be strong enough to withstand violent clashes yet hold a sharp edge. Early swords were made of iron that was pounded into shape by local blacksmiths. Later in the Middle Ages, steel, though very rare and expensive, became the favored metal. From the start of the Middle Ages to the finish, the sword's double edge was used as a slashing weapon and its tip as a piercing weapon.

One of the most useful sword innovations was the pommel, the round decorative object at the end of the grip. Swordsmen recognized that a pommel acted as a counterweight for balancing these heavy swords. Once introduced, the pommel allowed the knight to maneuver the sword more easily with less stress on his arm.

The power of the sword greatly increased when brandished from the back of a fast-charging horse. Knights spent a tremendous amount of money for their horses, and selected and trained them with great care to capitalize on their reliability and speed.

THE CHARGER

The horse was the single military component that differentiated the knight from all other medieval fighters; without one a fighter was not considered a knight. Warhorses, often called chargers, a term describing their use, were bred over the centuries for speed and stamina rather than for strength. Contrary to many contemporary accounts of enormous warhorses the size of one-ton Clydesdales or French Percherons, the preferred mount for a knight was the half-ton Arabian.

Horses were not outfitted in armor until the thirteenth century. Prior to that time, the maximum weight carried by a horse was rarely in excess of a 150-pound knight and his 60 or 70 pounds of armor and weaponry. A fully armored knight weighing in at 225 pounds or so demanded the speed and endurance of Arabians over the plodding strength of plow horses. The charger was not ridden to the battle, only during the battle. Consequently, demands made on it for maximum performance in the course of a battle were punctuated with brief moments for rest. During the waning years of the Middle Ages, plate armor was added to protect horses. Initially the armor covered only the

Knights fight each other with lances and swords, both lethal weapons on the battlefield when used on horseback.

❧ STIRRUPS AND KNIGHTS ❧

The medieval knight could not have performed great military feats on horseback without stirrups. Although these pieces of equestrian equipment pale as a symbol of medieval gallantry compared to armor, shields, and lances, they were crucial to success in battle.

The value of knights in battle was the shock effect they had of bearing down on the enemy. An effective charge had to be executed with speed, agility, and coordination. Before the introduction of the stirrup from China in the eighth century, riders clung to their steeds as best they could, often falling when their horses suddenly changed direction or stumbled. Stirrups became essential pieces of a knight's equipment because they welded the rider to the saddle.

Once the knight learned how to set his feet in the stirrups to maintain his balance, his hands were freed up to hold a shield in one and a lance in the other.

He also trained his horse to turn right and left with kicks to the horse's flanks with his boots firmly set in the stirrups. "Without the stirrup," muses medieval historian Melville Grosvenor in his book *The Age of Chivalry,* "no knight."

The stirrup allowed the knight to stay on his horse, freeing his hands for battle.

horse's head and chest, the two parts of the anatomy most susceptable during a charge against the enemy. Later, additional armor was added to protect the horse's flanks. More of the horse might have been protected but the additional weight reduced the horse's speed and agility. As a result Arabians did increase slightly in heft and strength.

Knights spent considerable time training their mounts for the rigors of battle. Mock battles were valuable to acquaint their horses with the disturbing sounds of clashing steel and shouting men in the midst of mass confusion. Preoccupied with a shield in the left hand and sword in the right, knights trained their mounts to turn, charge, and stop, guided only by the pressure of the rider's knees and spurs.

During times of peace, the only element of military equipment of value to the knight was his steed. Surviving knights returning home to act as civic administrators still needed their horses to perform their duties. The chargers were relieved of any armor and readied for less stressful chores, transporting their knights around castles and local villages at a leisurely pace.

THE CASTLE: A FORTIFIED HOME

The medieval castles that were owned by the wealthier knights were also considered weapons. The castle was the one piece of equipment, more than any other, that was required of every knight to justify his civic authority. Castles were rare in the eleventh century, but by the close of the Middle Ages, England, Germany, and France boasted more than ten thousand each.

The importance of the castle to each knight is reflected in its dual role as his family home and place of defense for the entire village in times of invasion. When an enemy army approached the castle walls, village bells signaled an invasion and summoned all villagers to gather weapons and food and hurry to the castle.

The castle was a heavy, imposing structure. Most were circumscribed by stone walls between twenty and forty feet high and seven to twenty feet thick. Designed for strength and strategic advantage, most were constructed on high ground, forcing attackers to carry their charge uphill. Some additional obstacles that invaders encountered were both wet and dry moats surrounding the exterior walls and crenellated towers, from the notched stone walls off which archers could shoot arrows at attackers below.

The villagers remained within the walls of the castle until the attackers departed or the villagers ran out of food and surrendered. The cost of feeding the besieged villagers fell to the knight, but any later repairs to the castle were done by the villagers. If invaders laid waste to peasants' fields and homes during a war, the knight reduced their obligations to him until they recovered from their losses.

Pictured is a castle in southern France built high on a hill. The castle served as both the knight's home and as a refuge in times of war.

Not until knights had acquired their armor and horses and had made their villages secure with their castles did they dare venture far from home to do battle. Yet when the call came from their lord to defend him in battle, the knights obeyed, as dictated by their oaths.

CHAPTER 3

THE KNIGHT AT WAR

The main duty of the knight's profession was fighting on the battlefield. It was also his principal source of income. Fighting in the service of his lord, who might be a local man or even the king, was the ultimate test of a knight's tactical training, quality of weaponry, and equestrian skills. Knights constituted the backbone of the army because they were trained professional soldiers and typically fought on horseback. For these reasons, they oversaw all aspects of a campaign. The clash of armies was what most knights lived for and for which they received their compensation, honor, and glory.

Few epic battles raged across the European countryside. Most were skirmishes over a right that had been violated, a piece of land that had been trespassed, or the intentional divergence of a stream. Most campaigns involved either a siege against a fortified castle and the ravaging of the hapless peasants' crops or a few clashes between drawn-up armies. If the battle was to be fought by two opposing armies on open fields, the most effective tactic for knights was the cavalry charge.

THE CAVALRY CHARGE

Between the tenth and fourteenth centuries, the knight reigned supreme on the battlefields of Europe. It was their heavy cavalry charge as a battle-winning tactic that brought them to preeminence. Medieval field armies were composed of a mix of mounted knights, archers, and sword-wielding infantrymen, and although the knights were the smallest contingent of the three, they were the most feared and the most lethal. More battles were decided by tactics of charging knights than by any other.

A cavalry charge consisted of hundreds and sometimes thousands of mounted knights racing toward each at

Knights on horseback engage in battle near a castle. The cavalry charge allowed knights to break through enemy lines.

full speed. When delivered in a well-timed and organized manner, a thundering charge of knights could break through the ranks of the enemy and overwhelm them with the chaos of trampling hooves, thrusting lances, and slashing swords. When swept down upon by knights, the foot soldiers were knocked about with such violence that they were incapacitated.

Bearing down those last two hundred yards, however, was dangerous. Enemy archers let loose a hail of arrows, which disrupted the orderly charge by unhorsing some knights and killing their mounts. In addition, if the enemy was well prepared, it might have scattered four-inch-long pointed iron spikes called caltrops in the path of the anticipated charge. When stepped on, these spikes hobbled the horses. Another enemy tactic was to dig a ditch in front of their frontline troops. They then embedded sharpened pikes into the ditch that killed the horses that fell onto them.

Knights surviving such an ordeal, however, were virtually unstoppable. Slamming into the enemy with lances

ॐ VICTORY AT ANY COST ॐ

Occasionally a commanding knight would do anything to gain a military advantage. Few stratagems to defeat an enemy can compare to the ruse employed by Sir John Marshall, the leader of soldiers inside the besieged Newbury Castle in England in 1152.

Following several months of siege warfare, Marshall proposed a one-day truce to Stephen, the leader of the attacking knights. The one day, Marshall explained, would give him an opportunity to consult his king about a possible surrender of the castle that might peacefully end the siege. If the enemy would agree to the truce, Marshall promised that he would ride off and make the proposal to the king. Suspecting a ruse, however, Stephen agreed to the one-day truce only if Marshall offered a guarantee in the form of a hostage, his five-year-old son, William. If anything should go awry, the boy would be executed.

Without hesitation, Marshall escorted William outside the castle gate where he turned the boy over to his enemy.

But Marshall had no intention of keeping his word. Instead, he took advantage of the truce to gather more provisions and fresh troops. When Stephen saw him return with more troops and provisions, he was outraged and announced to Marshall that he would soon see his young son slaughtered at the castle's main gate.

Denise Dersin reports in her book *What Life Was Like in the Age of Chivalry* that Marshall, defiant in the face of such a horrible sight, stoically shouted back to Stephen, "Do what you like with the boy. I still have the hammer and the forge to produce another one, even finer."

extended beyond their horses, knights pierced many combatants on the spot. Medieval historian Frances Gies conveys the impact of mounted knights riding down infantry:

> With the lance gripped under his arm and his body secured to his horse by saddle and stirrups, a knight could deliver his blow with the mass and strength of the horse united with his own, creating the sometimes overrated but nonetheless effective technique of shock combat.[10]

Then, drawing their swords, knights fought on, slashing at others as the flying hooves of their one-thousand-pound mounts trampled those unable to flee or cover themselves with their shields.

Under no circumstances did a knight voluntarily dismount to fight. Often, however, he was forced to do so if his horse was mortally wounded. Some knights were dragged off their rearing mounts by halberds, long-handled pikes with a hook at one end. Others were knocked off by agile, unarmed foot soldiers who were able to jump on the backs of the horses. When any of these situations occurred, the knight had no choice but to continue the fight on foot.

FIGHTING ON FOOT

On foot, the knight lost his advantage. Nonetheless, knights were trained to fight in this manner. While knights had the advantage of being encased in a suit of armor, they faced reduced maneuverability, in comparison to some of their adversaries. However, if both opponents were knights with similar equipment, the fight was more fair.

In cases of one-on-one combat, the fight might be fair if both knights used their broadswords—six-foot-long swords that required the knight to hold them with both hands. The strategy when facing an armored adversary was to attempt to execute a quick sword thrust to the neck of his opponent, by raising the sword high and driving the point downward at the neck where the helmet met the collar. Otherwise, the two men would thrust and parry until one knight was badly beaten, a sword broke, one was knocked to the ground, or someone simply ran away. In many cases, two exhausted knights agreed to quit and return to their camps.

Combat on foot sometimes became group combat. Occasionally two groups of adversaries organized to counter each other. When this occurred, one group formed a circle with their backs to the center. This formation allowed each knight to focus on the fighter in front of him without the distraction of constantly having to check his back. Sometimes, too, if the knights still had their shields, they would stand tightly packed together using their shields to form a protective wall.

One of the worst situations for an unhorsed knight was confronting a

Although trained to fight on horseback, knights were also very skilled in hand-to-hand combat, as this battle scene shows.

soldier without constraining armor who wielded a weapon capable of crushing his armor with blunt force. Challenged by an enemy with a large rock, a mace, or a flail—a wooden baton with an iron ball attached to one end by a short chain—the knight's chances were slim. Under such a disadvantage, a stunned knight would often surrender.

RANSOMING CAPTURED KNIGHTS

Neither a yeoman (a peasant farmer) nor a knight would pass on an opportunity to accept a defeated knight's overture to surrender. Most knights were from wealthy families that would willingly pay a ransom rather than see the master's corpse returned home slung over his horse's saddle.

Captured knights were worth more alive than dead. The ransoms demanded and received made many a yeoman's family wealthy. Of all sources of income, no matter what the warrior's position in society, the ransom of a wealthy prisoner was the most lucrative. The ransom of a high lord or even a king could reach astronomical figures—hence the term a "king's ransom." When the English king Richard I was captured in Austria in 1192, the ransom demanded for his safe return was 150,000 silver marks, the modern equivalent of tens of millions of dollars. The amount was so great that when Richard was released, he levied a special tax on all Englishmen to pay for his ransom. Generally the ransom reflected the worth of the family fortune, but occasionally the ransom was

Enemy soldiers take a king as prisoner. A king's ransom could command outrageous sums of money.

ture by a messenger carrying a ransom note and some personal artifact such as a ring or his sword as proof of the capture. Once the ransom note was received, the family either paid the money on the spot or asked for time to raise the necessary amount. In the latter case, the family carried the money under heavy guard to the castle holding the captured family member. Eleanor of Aquitaine, wife of King Henry II of England and mother of King Richard the Lion-Hearted, once raised her son's ransom and went to Austria herself to deliver it and accompany Richard back to England.

While awaiting delivery of the ransom, the code of chivalry required accommodations and food for captured knights that reflected their social status. Medieval writings report captured knights passing their time hunting with their captors, attending gala dinner parties, and exchanging stories and experiences with their host. In exchange for friendly and sumptuous accommodations, knights pledged not to attempt to escape.

Ransoming captured knights was a phenomenon of battles where warriors were engaged in a face-to-face struggle. Not all battles, however, pitted men against each other in this way. Many

negotiated downward and, on rare occasions, not even paid. The ransom for King Jean II of France, for example, was so enormous that the French never paid it and the king died of natural causes in captivity.

Captured knights, even if not kings, were worth keeping alive. A knight's family was notified of its master's cap-

knights attacked castles. When villagers and their knights took refuge within castle walls for protection, siege warfare was inevitable.

SIEGE WARFARE

When battlefield skirmishes turned sour for a hometown army, they and their families fled to the lord's castle for safety. As castles evolved from large homes to fortresses, they became military objectives. Although castles came in a variety of shapes and sizes, the majority were mammoth edifices reflecting a lord's social status and military prowess. For these reasons, invading armies generally knew where to find the local army.

The objective for attackers was to make their way into the castle one way or another, while the strategy for the besieged was to resist the attackers with equal resolve. Time was of the essence for both sides for different reasons; the besieged had a dwindling supply of food, while the besiegers were far from home and most knights were only obligated to stay for forty days.

⚜ A KNIGHT'S LOVE OF WAR ⚜

Some knights lost themselves in the passion of war. This extract from a twelfth-century writer describing one knight's poetic love of war is taken from Marc Bloch's book Feudal Society.

I love the gay Eastertide [Easter season], which brings forth leaves and flowers; and I love the joyous songs of the birds, re-echoing through the fields. But also I love to see, amidst the fields, a spread of tents and pavilions; and it gives me great joy to see, drawn up on the fields, knights and horses in battle array. And it delights me when the scouts scatter people and herds in their path; and I love to see them followed by a great number of men-at-arms; and my heart is filled with gladness when I see strong castles besieged, and the walls broken and overwhelmed, and the knights on the bank . . . with a line of strong stakes, interlaced. Maces, swords, helms [helmets] of different hues, shields that will be driven and shattered as soon as the fight begins; and many knights struck down together; and the horses of the dead and wounded roving at random. And when the battle is joined, let all good men of lineage think of naught but the breaking of heads and arms; for it is better to die than to be vanquished and live. I tell you, I find no such favor in food, or in wine, or in sleep, as in hearing the shout, 'On! On!' from both sides, and the neighing of steeds that have lost their riders, and the cries of 'Help! Help!'; in seeing men great and small go down on the grass . . . in seeing at last the dead, with the stumps of lances still in their sides.

The responsibility for designing and implementing strategies for conquering a castle fell to the senior knights. It was their job to figure out how to penetrate the castle walls using their expertise and experience. In most cases, knights had many strategies from which to choose: blockade the castle and starve the inhabitants into submission, employ a clever ruse or a bribe to gain entry, scale the walls with ladders, breach the walls, or tunnel under them. Of these, the last two were the most dramatic and difficult.

Breaching walls was generally accomplished by employing either massive battering rams or catapults. The battering ram was made from a large tree. On one end was carved a point that was then sheathed with a heavy iron tip. Soldiers then built a mobile carriage, laid the ram on it, and wheeled the contraption toward the wooden doors of the castle or the weakest section of the wall.

As they approached the castle wall, the operators of the ram were attacked from above by defenders who hurled all manner of bone-crushing debris down on them. For protection, the operators built a wooden shelter covered with rawhide and heavy wood planks under which they would work. After the ram was rolled under the shelter, it was removed from the carriage and slung on parallel rows of chains that were bolted to a stationary frame extending the length of the ram. Once the

frame was set in place against a gate, soldiers pulled back the ram resting on the cradle of chains and swung it forward, crashing it against the gate. The ram was swung over and over until it smashed through the gate.

The drawback to the ram was the necessity of using it in close proximity to the castle walls. For this reason, catapults capable of hurling stones great distances were preferred because they could operate from a safe distance. Of several designs, the trebuchet was the most effective and safest for the attacking army. The trebuchet worked on the principle of counterweights: a long pivoting wooden beam with a heavy weight on one end and a sling containing a heavy stone on the other. When the weight was dropped, the sling flew up with great force, launching the stone toward the castle wall. A trebuchet with a sixty-foot-long pivoting beam was capable of pounding a section of wall with two-hundred-pound stones from two hundred feet away.

UNDERGROUND SIEGE WARFARE

Stones smashing gates and walls were dramatic but not always the most effective means of subduing an enemy. A very different kind of siege warfare, one that was invisible and silent, was the mining of passageways under the castle walls.

Mining was one of the best ways to breach a wall, though it was the least favored method because it was slow and tedious. A tunnel was dug from the besieger's lines and underneath a section of the wall. To prevent the tunnel from collapsing while it was being dug, heavy wooden timbers propped it up from within. Once a mine was of sufficient size, typically the height of a man and ten feet wide, and it extended completely under the foundation of a castle wall, the timbers were wrapped in pigskins and bacon and then set on fire. Once the wooden props had burned away, the section of wall above the mine was no longer supported and it collapsed into the tunnel, producing a large breach through which invading knights scrambled.

The only countermeasure to mining was countermining. Suspicious castle defenders placed pans of water on the ground and watched for ripples in the water caused by the vibrations of miners' picks and shovels. When vibrations were discovered, the direction of the mine was determined by placing more pans of water around the suspected area and observing which ones vibrated and which did not.

Once a mine location was confirmed, a countermine was excavated from inside the castle to intercept the incoming mine. When the countermine broke through into the invaders' mine, a chaotic fight in the

Knights besiege a castle, looking for ways to gain entry.

dark broke out. Occasionally, if a castle was near a river or stream, a more effective countermeasure to stop miners was to divert a stream into the mine, drowning all inside.

No matter what strategy of destroying castle walls was employed, it was hard, slow, and costly. If any other way of gaining access to the interior was possible, it was tried. Paying a traitor a large sum of gold to smuggle invaders in sometimes did the trick, but more often some sort of deception was employed.

CONQUEST BY GUILE AND DECEPTION

Knights in charge of sieges always looked for deceptive ways to entice the enemy to foolishly open their gates. In the summer of 1356, the Duke of Lancaster, England, landed in France with his army for the purpose of laying siege to the castle at Rennes on the Brittany peninsula. As summer gave way to fall, which in turn gave way to winter, unsuccessful English soldiers clamored to return to England, forcing the duke to gather his council of elder knights to discuss their options. Understanding that the inhabitants of the besieged castle were near starvation, one knight proposed an imaginative ruse to gain entry.

The English raided the surrounding farms, gathering a herd of four thousand pigs and driving them before the walls of the starving French. The English hoped that the hungry French would come out to gather the pigs, at which time the English mounted knights would storm through the open gates. The French noblemen inside, however, were every bit the match of the English when it came to clever chicanery.

In a masterly countermove, the French suspended a pig by its hind legs above a drawbridge near the herd outside. The squeals of the dangling pig attracted the attention of the herd, which headed for the gate. At just the right moment, the drawbridge was lowered and the suspended pig was let go to run into the castle, which it did, now followed by enough pigs to feed the besieged population for months.

On occasion, even well-born knights were asked to make disgusting sacrifices for their king. In 1203, six knights of the besieging French king Philip Augustus volunteered to gain access to the Château Gaillard by crawling through a latrine trench that drained outside the walls. Once inside and posing as local residents, the infiltrators succeeded in lowering the drawbridge to admit the rest of their force.

Fighting at castle walls or on the open battlefield caused severe wounds to many knights. Part of the knight's responsibility was to tend to

wounds because doctors did not accompany knights into battle.

TREATING BATTLEFIELD WOUNDS

Thousands of knights swinging swords, maces, battle-axes, and war hammers created unimaginable battlefield carnage. In March 1461, for example, between twenty-two thousand and twenty-eight thousand men were speared, axed, and crushed to death on the battlefield of Towton, England. Shannon Novak, a forensic archaeologist who excavated the medieval battlefield, notes, "The level of trauma was surprising. Some of these men from Towton have 13 wounds to the head. There were also many different types of wounds present on single individuals."[11] Such butchery made

Many knights were killed or severely injured in battle. Some even died from infected wounds off the battlefield.

battlefield medicine a necessary part of the job for many knights.

Lack of cleanliness caused major and minor wounds to become infected. One of the most common remedies, and the remedy of choice for saving lives, was to sacrifice the infected limb. A few knights received primitive training for amputation in their local butcher shops. A successful amputation was not particularly complicated, but the key was speed. One medieval account recommended, "Have an excellent assistant who has a grip that a lion would struggle to break free from and have the sharpest butcher's knife known to man."[12] Lacking a butcher's knife, a knight used his sharpest blade to hack through muscle and bone in a single swing if possible. The bleeding stump was immediately tied off with a tight leather strap to staunch the bleeding and then cauterized with fire to disinfect it.

Not all knights were keen to lose their leg. In 1403, one knight, Pero Niño, who faced the despairing proposition of the loss of his wounded leg, argued instead to have a hot iron brought to him to cauterize the wound in hopes of saving the leg. According to a witness, "They heated an iron, big as a squirrel, white hot. Pero Niño took the glowing iron and himself moved it over his leg from one end of the wound to the other."[13] Remarkably, the leg healed.

At least a few knights in each army had some experience using sutures to sew up sword and lance gashes. Sutures made from animal intestines, silk, and wool were often effective in preventing death caused by massive hemorrhaging. Most of the needles used to pull the sutures through the skin were made of glass and sharpened bone, though a few were made of steel.

If wounded knights were lucky to be fighting near home, their squires loaded them on a wagon or draped them over their horse to ride home for better medical attention. Often simply cleaning a wound in the clean and warm environment of their homes saved many lives. Such comforts, however, were not available for knights fighting far from home, and no knights fought farther from home than those who participated in the Crusades.

CHAPTER 4

CRUSADING KNIGHTS

In 1095, roughly the halfway point in the history of medieval knighthood, knights' warring responsibilities took a dramatic turn. For roughly the next two hundred years, they would be required to leave behind their relatively provincial military squabbles to lay siege to towns and cities thousands of miles away in the Holy Land, a narrow strip of land along the eastern Mediterranean Sea. This territory, sacred to Christians, had been invaded and occupied by invading Muslim armies.

For the first time in European history, a holy war unified all knights. Putting aside most of their local bickering in the face of an alien religion that threatened the towns and cities where Jesus once lived, knights united under the banner of Christianity to liberate sacred lands. Far from home, absent for very long periods, and fighting a foe culturally different from them, knightly obligation faced its most formidable foe. This sudden refocusing of the knightly profession was a historical event that medieval historian Frances Gies calls "the largest single event in the annals of knighthood."[14]

A HOLY CALL TO ARMS

The call to crusade against the Muslim armies went out in 1095 when Pope Urban II addressed a church council in the French city of Clermont. Seated before cardinals and bishops and French nobility, Urban made his pitch for a full-scale crusade of knights by driving emotions to a frenzy when he said,

It is the imminent peril threatening you and all the faithful which has brought us here. From the confines of Jerusalem a horrible tale has gone forth . . . an accursed race, a race utterly alienated from God . . . has invaded the lands of Christians and has depopulated

This stained glass window in a French church idealizes the crusading knight as he battles Muslim armies occupying the Holy Land.

them by sword, pillage, and fire. On whom, therefore, is the labor of avenging these wrongs and of recovering these territories incumbent, if not upon you? Enter upon the road to the Holy Sepulcher [Jesus' tomb]; wrest that land from the wicked race, and subject it to yourselves.[15]

When Urban completed his exhortation for war, a chant arose from the crowd— "*Deus volt, Deus volt, Deus volt,*" meaning "God wills it." As each knight set out for his long journey across Europe to the Holy Land, each swore an oath to remain faithful to Christianity and to abide by the code of chivalry. With that oath, each then tore up bits of clothing into strips and sewed them on their shields and cloaks in the form of the cross. Fulcher of Chartres was one historian who witnessed this act and declared, "O how fitting it was, how pleasing to us all to see these crosses."[16]

A BRUTAL FIRST CRUSADE

The First Crusade (seven more would follow) to liberate Jerusalem was a siren call for Europe's knights. A campaign to a foreign land reportedly rich in gold, silver, and precious jewels fired many knights' imaginations with thoughts of rich ransoms and opulent spoils of war. Two years after the pope's summons to war, four thousand knights along with seven thousand infantry and eleven thousand archers from across Europe joined the initial campaign now known to historians as the First Crusade.

The lure of riches faded quickly, however, as the army made its long trek across Europe. They marched from France, through northern Italy, then

As crusaders fought their way to the Holy Land, Christian chivalry faded and pillaging became the norm.

across eastern Europe and finally through Turkey. They covered hundreds of miles through scorching heat and also deep snow in the mountain passes. The crusaders ran out of fresh water on numerous occasions, and according to one survivor, some were reduced to drinking their own urine, animal blood, and water drawn from sewage ditches. Obtaining food presented similar problems. Most was purchased from local peoples along the route at exorbitant prices until money ran low. Christian historians accompanying the crusaders hoping to write of their glorious acts of Christian chivalry instead reported desperate acts of pillaging and plundering from peasants to stay alive. Many abandoned the crusade and shamefully crept back home.

In 1098, roughly ten thousand remaining crusaders of the initial twenty-eight thousand gathered at Constantinople, Turkey's largest city located at the confluence of the Aegean and Black seas, to rest before journeying to Jerusalem. Heading south, the first target of the crusaders was the fortress city of Nicaea, which was conquered following a vicious siege. Next was Antioch, a strongly defended Turkish city that took a seven-month siege before it fell. At this juncture, no opposition stood between the crusaders and their goal of Jerusalem.

The attack of Jerusalem commenced in the summer of 1099. The entire city was protected by high walls and stout gates that crusaders eventually scaled. What then took place was a horrid spectacle. The historian Fulcher of Chartres who accompanied the crusaders wrote a lengthy commentary of the carnage that took the lives of an estimated seventy thousand Muslims. The place of the bloodiest carnage was the Temple of Solomon, and Fulcher was there to provide this eyewitness account:

> A great fight took place in the court and porch of the temple, where they were unable to escape from our gladiators [knights]. Many fled to the roof of the temple of Solomon, and were shot with arrows, so that they fell to the ground dead. In this temple almost ten thousand were killed. Indeed, if you had been there you would have seen our feet colored to our ankles with the blood of the slain. But what more shall I relate? None of them were left alive; neither women nor children were spared.[17]

THE SIEGE OF ENTIRE CITIES

The sieges of large cities such as Nicaea, Antioch, and Jerusalem were significantly more complex and difficult than the sieges of castles. Knights experienced with and trained in the tactics of overwhelming a castle reeled

❧ LEARNING HISTORY FROM ☙ THE BAYEUX TAPESTRY

Following the Battle of Hastings in 1066 between the invading French and the English, French weavers created a tapestry that pictorially portrays the battle. This tapestry, which resides in the French city of Bayeux, is viewed by many historians as one of the most unusual historical documents ever created. This remarkable tapestry, 231 feet long and 20 inches wide, identifies the major figures of the battle, presents scenes of combat, shows battlefield strategies and army positioning, and provides historians with a wealth of depictions of mounted knights, their armor, and castle architecture at that time. Of all depictions, however, those of knights' armor and weapons are the most intriguing.

Because of the relatively early date of the battle that the tapestry depicts, historians have concluded from many segments of battle scenes that most knights at that time rode into battle with only chain mail and a helmet to protect their bodies; no plate armor is in evidence. Others are depicted without any armor whatsoever. Those with chain mail are covered from neck to knee, and the helmets are slightly conical in shape and without faceplates. None of the horses are shown in armor, although some are caparisoned, draped neck to tail with colorful low-hanging blankets.

The tapestry depicts a wide variety of weaponry. Almost all mounted knights carried a shield, always in the left hand, and a lance in the right hand. Some knights carried lances with small pennants bearing their coat of arms. Those without shield and lance are shown with a wooden club and a few carry a mace, a wooden club with an iron knob on the end.

when confronted with walled cities the size of Jerusalem.

The principal impediments to besieging city walls were their enormity and the density of buildings that lay immediately outside of them. At the siege of Jerusalem, for example, crusading knights encountered the city's circuit wall, which was two and a half miles long and forty feet high. Individual stones, many exceeding one ton, were much too large to displace with battering rams. The use of catapults was also rendered ineffective because no open fields within the range of catapults could be found to launch stone projectiles. Furthermore, determining the weakest sections to attack was impossible because no knight had ever seen the interior of the city walls, which was necessary to discover the weakest point.

Other formidable disadvantages also faced the crusaders. Large cities had multiple sources of water and ample food supplies. The siege of Antioch, for example, ended when the wall was breached, not because of surrender due to starvation. Many of the cities also constructed secret tunnels running between

Crusaders conquer the city of Antioch in 1098. Taking a city was far more difficult than laying siege to a castle.

the city and the outside. The tunnels were used to resupply beleaguered defenders and to orchestrate quick hit-and-run attacks against enemy soldiers.

Sieges thousands of miles from home took their toll on besiegers as well as the besieged. Fulcher of Chartres grimly reported details of food shortages for crusaders at Antioch, "Both the rich and the poor were desolate from hunger, and the knights ate shoots of bean seeds growing in the fields and thistles . . . also horses, asses, and camels and dogs and rats."[18] At another battle, Fulcher noted that things got even worse: "They cut pieces of the buttocks of the Saracens [Muslims] . . . which they cooked."[19]

UNCHECKED SLAUGHTER

The knightly code of chivalry, which was conceived to check the reckless, violent behavior of knights, was not evidenced in the Holy Land. Contemporary medieval historians as well as chroniclers accompanying the warriors noted the lack of ethical conduct of many knights far from home.

Chroniclers of the Crusades recorded horrific examples of senseless slaughter. The worst of it included the mutilation of Muslim slaves while still alive, the slaughter of captives at Antioch, the mounting of Muslim heads on pikes, and even the use of heads as missiles catapulted over city walls. Helpless townspeople who had swallowed their gold in hopes of

❧ THE MASSACRE AT WORMS ❧

Not all knights heading off on the First Crusade embodied chivalric principles. In May of 1096, the crusading German knight Count Emich and his troops on their way to the Holy Land swept through the village of Worms pulling Jews from their homes and giving them the choice of conversion to Christianity or death.

Stephen A. Dafoe's article "A Slaughter of Innocents" posted on the Web site Templar History, *at www.templarhistory.com, cites Emich as explaining his actions by saying,* "Since they were the race responsible for the death and crucifixion of Jesus, they deserved nothing better than conversion or death."

What followed, however, was far worse. Chronicler of the Crusades, Robert of Aix, reported part of the grisly affair quoted in Paul Halsall's "Emich and the Slaughter of the Rhineland Jews", *in the* Internet Medieval Sourcebook *located at www.fordham.edu:*

But Emich and the rest of his band held a council and, after sunrise, attacked the Jews in the hall with arrows and lances. Breaking the bolts and doors, they killed the Jews, about seven hundred in number, who in vain resisted the force and attack of so many thousands.

They killed the women, also, and with their swords pierced tender children of whatever age and sex. The Jews, seeing that their Christian enemies were attacking them and their children, and that they were sparing no age, likewise fell upon one another, brother, children, wives, and sisters, and thus they perished at each other's hands. Horrible to say, mothers cut the throats of nursing children with knives and stabbed others, preferring them to perish thus by their own hands rather than to be killed by the weapons of the uncircumcised [Christians]."

hiding it from their conquerors were disemboweled and their gold removed. Neither age nor sex mattered; the slaughter seemed indiscriminate.

Muslims were not the only ones to experience the wrath of crusaders. Knights passing through the German town of Worms during the First Crusade murdered more than seven hundred Jews who refused to convert to Christianity. Christians, too, were targeted. Long before the crusaders reached the Holy

Land, some knights pillaged their way across the landscape, killing peasant farmers who tried to protect their livestock from slaughter. And once in the Holy Land, the lure of plunder often set one crusading band against another in deadly combat to establish the right to loot towns and villages.

Contemporary historians are split on their explanations for the knights' abysmal failure to adhere to their chivalric code. Some say the code did not apply to the non-Christian Muslims, while others believe that high-minded notions of chivalry were largely a sham regardless of where the knights traveled or against whom they fought.

THE COSTS OF CRUSADING

The financial obligations of a crusading knight were stiff. Paying for his and his squires' food, equipment, and incidental expenses for years at a time was a hefty obligation. Over the course of nearly two hundred years, paying for the fighting gradually shifted, dramatically altering the profile of the crusading knight. During the early Crusades, knights were obligated to serve forty days and agreed to accept the spoils of war and promises of land and future compensation for time beyond the forty days. Few knights found fair compensation.

A group of knights buys the right of exemption from fighting in the Holy Land with a large sum of money.

After one hundred years of crusading, roughly at the start of the Fourth Crusade, fewer knights were willing to fight for plunder and unspecified wages. Knights asked to march to the Holy Land preferred to purchase their release by paying a sum of money to the king called a scutage, which he then used to hire mercenaries. Most mercenaries were common knights with little money and limited battlefield experience. They fought as long as they were paid and departed for home the moment the money ran out.

Mercenary knights were costly. Just paying for their transportation by boat from Venice to the Holy Land at the outset of the Fourth Crusade in 1102 was the staggering sum of eighty-five thousand German marks—four marks per horse and two marks per man. This total amount would be roughly equivalent to $20 million today. Combat pay for each man was often disbursed for ninety-day periods. The archers and foot soldiers were the least expensive. One chronicler reported that they were paid about 1,000 Italian ducats, roughly the modern equivalent of about $300, but a squire received 2,400 and a full knight 5,000. A senior knight, however, who assumed responsibility for organizing and leading a large contingency received 12,000 ducats.

Far from home after the first, second, or third ninety-day period, knights often failed to receive their promised payments from kings. Desperate to keep the troops on the battle line, kings and nobles encouraged the knights to pillage as a form of payment.

PILLAGING TO PAY EXPENSES

The prolonged Crusades left rulers with few options but to pass on the costs of the war to the knights and their men. The custom was to allow the fighting men to claim the lion's share of the spoils of war that were taken from the homes of the wealthy. These spoils typically included gold, jewelry, and religious relics. Towns and castles often yielded tens of millions of ducats in coins and treasure. For a crusading army of twelve to fifteen thousand, the two to three thousand or so knights would claim at least half the spoils.

Pillaging poor villagers was a viable option for knights running short on money and food. European kings and their lords were willing to turn a blind eye to the obvious violations of the rules of chivalry that forbade inflicting injury on poor and innocent civilians. This irresponsible policy caused kings and lords to lose all control of their thieving knights.

Any sense of order and ethical behavior within bands of crusading knights when they departed Europe for the Holy Land quickly deteriorated. Church leaders concerned that knights were failing to honor the code of chivalry established military orders of knights that required each man to live the austere life of a monk.

KNIGHTLY MONKS

Near the aftermath of the bloody First Crusade in 1099, the first religious organizations to function as military orders were founded in response to greed-driven knights. Unlike their predecessors, these crusading knights embraced the code of chivalry. To strengthen their connection to Christianity, they swore the same vows as monks to practice obedience, chastity, and poverty.

The first orders of knightly monks were called the Knights Templar, whose charter was to fulfill a monk's religious obligations while providing for the protection and care of Christian pilgrims traveling to and within the Holy Land. The Templars were soon followed by a host of similar orders, most notably the Teutonic Knights and the Hospitallers.

To prevent knightly monks from becoming tempted by greed and corruption, each order had a set of rigid rules limiting their worldly possessions. In return for their acceptance of poverty, the bishop of Jerusalem offered them land on which to build their monasteries,

This Knight Templar was part of a military order established by the church to encourage the revival of chivalry.

food and clothing, and a guarantee of re-mission of all sins. With these offerings, knightly monks had no motive to pillage.

These military orders were greeted with enormous enthusiasm by the laypeople and the clergy in both the Holy Land and Europe, as is evidenced in this manuscript dated 1118:

> In this same year, certain noble men of knightly rank, religious men, de-voted to God and fearing him, bound themselves to Christ's serv-ice in the hands of the Lord Patri-arch. They promised to live in per-petuity as regular canons, without possessions, under vows of chastity, poverty, and obedience. . . . Their primary duty was that of protect-ing the roads and routes against the attacks of robbers and brigands. This they did especially in order to safeguard pilgrims.[20]

The lives of knights who joined these military orders were far too Spartan for most knights. At the other end of the spectrum, some crusading knights saw opportunity for great wealth. Rather than becoming knightly monks or pil-laging, these knights recognized that a fortune could be earned by trading and operating a variety of businesses.

KNIGHTS AS TRADERS AND BUSINESSMEN

As major cities in the Holy Land fell to the crusaders, a handful of knights showed an interest in exchanging their suits of armor for the elegant clothing of wealthy traders, businessmen, and bankers. European traders had earlier looked to the eastern Mediterranean as a source of business, and following the First Crusade, some entrepreneurial knights set about controlling foreign com-merce, trade routes, and interest rates.

Groups of knights who had become familiar with the alien culture of the eastern Mediterranean organized trade with Europe. From Europe they loaded seagoing freighters with cloth, horses, armor, silver, and leather in exchange for a long list of goods demanded by lords and ladies in Europe. Freighters returned with their holds loaded with exotic foods such as dates, salted mus-sels, honey desserts, ostrich eggs, and exotic spices like pepper, cloves, ginger, saffron, and cinnamon. Stylish women looked forward to crates filled with ex-pensive jewelry made of ivory, pearls, and malachite, and elegant gowns of colorful silks, brocades, and satins.

Knights who preferred to spend their time trading rather than fighting made fortunes. As their wealth grew, some put their money to work by loaning it to pil-grims on their way to the Holy Land, to other knights preferring to pay the scu-tage rather than fight, and to kings in need of more money to hire mercenaries for future Crusades. Knights function-ing as bankers hit the jackpot in 1145 when the French king Louis VII put out the call for the Second Crusade and bor-

☙ THE PILGRIMAGE ❧

The main reason for the Crusades was to protect Christians traveling to the Holy Land and to recapture lands and monuments sacred to them on their visits. Who were these people who required protection by knights and what motivated their journeys? The church encouraged as many people as possible to make these long journeys, called pilgrimages, because some believed that such pilgrimages showed penance for sins they may have committed and would win them forgiveness from God. Others went as acts of thanksgiving for some good fortune they had received or for recovery from a life-threatening disease. Many pilgrims visited shrines scattered throughout Europe, but the most sacred pilgrimage was to the Holy Land and specifically to Jerusalem.

Although medieval pilgrimages to the Holy Land were not intended to be just for the nobility, few others had the money or the time to make a pilgrimage that might take up to three months if they chose to walk. Anyone who went on such a journey, regardless of income, placed the operations of his home, fields, livestock, and businesses at risk.

The value of the pilgrimage for the most devout pilgrims was the suffering experienced along the way. These pilgrims, although a minority, believed that by suffering along the way they were demonstrating to God the sincerity of their religious commitment. Some took the pilgrimage so seriously that they wore the coarsest clothing possible so that it scratched and chafed their skin. Some even traveled the entire journey barefoot, carrying a staff to assist them when they became lame. The more they suffered, they believed, the greater the likelihood that God would look favorably upon them.

rowed money to pay for it. The arrangement worked out so well that all of the succeeding Crusades were funded in part by loans from banking houses owned by knights. According to historian Scott J. Beem, knights "provided shipping and even built their own fleets and developed and harnessed an advanced array of banking institutions, and provided advice and guidance to kings and upper nobility."[21]

For knights attracted to the fighting, however, hard times came when the intermittent Crusades reached periods of peace. During these times, fighting knights kept their battle skills sharp and coin purses full by participating in mock battles called tournaments.

CHAPTER 5

TOURNAMENTS

Tournaments were one of the most violent and dangerous of medieval sports. They were a combination of bloody warfare and entertainment. Tournaments were festive public spectacles that presented knights with opportunities to hone their fighting skills. The tournament evolved over time from the eleventh century, when they were little more than reckless clashes between warriors, to the fourteenth century, when they became well-organized, festive social events.

Honing their fighting skills was only one of many incentives. Profit was another. Tournaments offered knights opportunities to earn money by defeating adversaries and to find employment by displaying their military prowess before lords who might be shopping for warriors. Tournaments were also a way for many young knights to test their novice battle skills.

The color and pageantry of these social events masked their violent nature.

Nonetheless, the impression left by many medieval writers is that tournaments allowed wives and families an opportunity to dress up in fine clothes and put on a display of courtly leisure and polished manners while the men displayed their athletic skills and savage aggression.

THE MELEE

The earliest tournaments, long before they became associated with social pageantry, were more closely akin to real battles. There were few rules and much blood. Known initially as melees, these events began in the eleventh century and quickly spread in popularity across Europe.

Melees were waged between two groups of knights. Each group had between twenty-five and one hundred warriors. The groups in a melee might be determined by nationality—for example the French versus the English—or more simply, by village loyalties. It did not matter that the men they fought might be their countrymen or friends; in the melee, they were the enemy.

The site of the melee encompassed several square miles of territory and was located between two towns. It often included pastureland, crops, vineyards, and even small villages. The property and welfare of the peasant bystanders was not a major concern, and often these people were caught up in the mayhem of the melee, to the detriment of their lands and dwellings.

Once a melee began, it carried on all day, unrestricted by rules or mediation by referees. The only safe zone was an area called a recess, where knights could take temporary refuge to repair armor or tend to wounds. Unlike other forms of sporting combat intended for entertainment, the fighting in a melee was real, and knights used the armor and weapons they employed in actual battle against enemy forces.

This scene of parading knights in armor shows the color and pageantry of the tournament, a popular social event.

Hundreds of spectators gather for a melee, a tournament with few rules and plenty of blood.

Without referees, these free-for-alls, fought on horseback and on foot, were so violent that the only distinction between them and war was the acknowledgment that they were considered by contestants to be a sport and that temporary rest could be found in the recess. Sixty knights were killed in one French tournament, while in another a knight killed his own son. Even royalty suffered loss; the brother of the English king Richard died at a tournament in Paris when he was thrown from his horse and trampled to death.

In spite of many deaths, killing was not the objective. Knights came principally to sharpen their fighting skills and make some money. Victors who killed their enemy took his horse and stripped the dead man of his armor and weapons. Losers who surrendered forfeited their horse and armor and paid a ransom. For many losing knights, such losses might mean the loss of land and village businesses.

Alarmed at the number of deaths that occurred during melees, the church banned the competitions in the mid–twelfth century and refused to bury those killed in them. One French monk was reported as saying, "Those who fall in the melee will go to hell."[22] Despite the ban, the melee continued in a more civilized format. Called the tournament, it was both socially more acceptable and regulated to reduce the mortality rate.

TOURNAMENTS

Around the beginning of the thirteenth century, kings joined the pope to curtail the unchecked carnage of the melee; too many good knights were being killed. Rules were instituted for the first time to preserve the demonstrations of combat skills without the flagrant loss of life. The civility that rules brought was soon accompanied by spectators, primarily the nobility, who saw the regulated tournament as a form of elegant entertainment complete with elaborate festive decorations, minstrels, wagering, and banquets.

Tournaments retained the basic battlefield tactics found in the melee: one army attacked another but with blunted swords, and more knights surrendered instead of being killed. The actual tournament began with the "lance charge," in which armored opponents collided on horseback. The two forces clashed, often at great cost to men and mounts. Then, when the respective charges had ground to a halt, the two sides would begin to pound one another, riding to and fro, jockeying for position. The engagement became a swirling mass of horses and riders with participants hacking and slashing at one another in an attempt to win the advantage.

While skirmishes ranged up and down the open fields, men and women of the nobility sat in elevated seats along the sidelines to enjoy the action. Spectators made bets while consuming ample food and drink provided by the host. According to one twelfth-century chronicler known only by his first name, Jean, these tournaments were indeed gala events:

> Banners were unfurled; the field was so full of them that the sun was concealed. There was great noise and din. All knights strove to strike well. Then you would hear such a clash of lances that the earth was strewn with fragments, such that the horses could not advance further. Great was the tumult upon the field. Each corps of the fighters cheered its banner.[23]

The festive air of tournaments did not change the basic brutish nature of the

Less brutal than a melee, tournaments provided entertainment for nobility, who observed from the sidelines and made bets.

DISTINGUISHING FRIEND FROM FOE

Medieval knights did not go into tournaments (or battle) with uniforms that identified the opposition. In the midst of a melee or tournament, when hundreds of knights and horses fell, distinguishing friend from foe was a daunting task. Accidental killings of friends became an added liability to battling knights.

Fighting in close quarters both on horseback and on foot, a knight's life might be lost or spared at the blink of an eye depending upon another knight's ability to identify him. To make a quick but certain identification, knights began painting their helmets and shields with large colorful symbols, called coats of arms, to identify them from all others.

event. A knight could gain or lose a fortune with a single swing of a sword. In the heat of a fray, with knights in full armor and faces hidden behind visors, recognizing whom to strike and whom to assist was often impossible. To enhance quick identification of friend and foe, a form of battlefield identity evolved.

Each coat of arms had three unique components: the colors, a prominent bold symbol called the cadency mark, and a geometric design called the charge. As the use of coats of arms evolved, each of the three components acquired symbolic meaning. As for colors, yellow denoted generosity, silver—

sincerity, black—consistency, blue—truth, and red—strength in battle. The cadency mark often featured the lion, denoting great courage; the horse, showing a commitment to serve king and country; or the trumpet, denoting readiness for leading an attack. The charge commonly displayed geometric designs such as the cross to signify the Christian faith, multiple bars indicating the number of sons in a knight's family, and broad bands meant to symbolize large landholdings.

One of the responsibilities of each knight heading into a tournament or battle was learning quickly to recognize the coats of arms of his compatriots to avoid the tragic mishap of killing them. Over time, each coat of arms was handed down to one's sons and became associated with a single family. Some coats of arms, especially those of the king or a powerful lord, were recognized by all knights. A conversation among spectators from the thirteenth century highlights people's familiarity with coats of arms:

> Do you see that knight yonder with a gold band across the middle of his red shield? That is Sir Roderick. And do you see that other one, who has an eagle and a

౿ THE SIGNIFICANCE OF HERALDRY ౭

Heraldry, the rules and traditions governing the use of coats of arms, played a vital role in the outcome of both tournaments and battles. For knights fighting in full armor with their faces hidden behind helmets, the coat of arms emblazoned on shields, a horse's caparison, and war banners helped them distinguish friend from foe in the confusion of battle.

The coat of arms could only be awarded by the king and only received by a knight. To put an end to unauthorized uses of coats of arms and to ensure that each was unique, in 1483 the English king Richard III instituted the Herald's College where coats of arms were officially registered in a great book. From that time forward, only knights with letters from the king were granted the honor of creating their coats of arms and painting them on their equipment.

Once the right to create and use a coat of arms was decreed, it had to be designed and approved by the Herald's College before it could be displayed. Generally, the designer of the coat of arms selected the colors, a main symbol such as an animal or other object, various vertical, horizontal, or diagonal stripes, and possibly a motto, which could be emblazoned on the bottom. Two of the more well-known mottos once used by English royalty were *Hon Y Soit Qui Mal Y Pense,* meaning "Shame to him who evil thinks," and *Dieu et Mon Droit,* meaning "God and My Right."

dragon painted side-by-side upon his shield? That is the son of the team of Aragon, who has come to this land in search of glory and renown. And do you see that one beside him bearing a shield with a leopard painted on the green background on one part, and the other half is azure blue? That is the well beloved Ignaurez.[24]

Going into tournament or battle bearing well-respected coats of arms could prevent one's death but could also be a liability. Knights scanned the enemy formations looking for well-known coats of arms on knights whose capture might bring a great ransom or whose death might bring personal prestige. Capturing and carrying home a shield or helmet bearing a well-respected coat of arms was an object of pride used to decorate a knight's great hall or castle entry room.

JOUSTS

The elaborate tournaments that dominated for many centuries began to lose popularity as the smaller-scale joust emerged. Set in a small venue, spectators enjoyed the contest from grandstand seats. The joust differed significantly from the tournament because it involved just two contestants on horseback, each attempting to kill or unhorse the other with a lance.

At the earliest jousting tournaments, contestants spurred their horses toward one another with their lances pointed at the chest of their opponent, each attempting to skewer the other and knock him off his horse. Once on the ground, if still alive, the unhorsed knight was at a distinct disadvantage because rules allowed the mounted warrior to run him down, trample him, or spear him with his lance. After many deaths occurred from direct lance hits that pierced chest armor, safeguards evolved requiring the tips of lances to be fitted with a three-pronged end called a coronal. This end was designed to distribute the force of the impact, thereby preventing the weapon from penetrating a knight's armor.

By the end of the fourteenth century, jousting became even more refined with the introduction of more safety features. The first feature was a barrier separating the two horses. Called a tilt barrier, it prevented charging horses from colliding head-on. Initially it was nothing more than a rope hung with fabric that separated the thundering horses, but later it evolved into a sturdier six-foot-tall wooden barrier that horses could not push across. The second refinement was the creation of wooden lances with a thin neck near the coronal that snapped when contact was made with an opponent's shield or chest armor. A knight who snapped his lance on an opponent was declared the winner.

Toward the end of the Middle Ages, when knights were no longer killed or seriously injured, points were awarded

Melees and tournaments gave way to jousting, which was smaller in scale and involved only two contestants on horseback.

to determine the winner. The rules were simple. Landing a clean hit to the center boss of the shield and shattering the lance or unhorsing an opponent scored the most points. Fewer points were awarded for striking the outer part of the shield and for deflecting lance blows. After two combatants completed three to six tilts against each other, the knight with the most points was awarded the prize money.

ALTERNATIVES TO VIOLENT SPORTS

To reduce bloody conflict among knights and yet continue the tradition of equestrian and combat skills, several alternatives to violent sports were introduced. One of the most popular alternatives was the *Pas d'Armes,* or Passage of Arms. In this event, one knight or group of knights defended a geographic feature, such as a bridge or

As an alternative to bloody conflict, a popular sport involved a knight tilting at a shield with his lance.

crossroads, against another knight or group of knights. These combats were called *combats à plaisance,* meaning "combats for pleasure." And since the contests were not intended to injure anyone, the swords were made of either wood or iron with blunted edges. Furthermore, *combats à plaisance* prohibited the ransoming of captured knights.

A second popular test of a knight's riding skills was the *quintain,* a game requiring a knight on horseback to use a lance to tilt with a target. In one of the most popular, a knight passed a lance through an iron loop and tilted at a shield, and in another the knight charged a dummy warrior suspended from a swinging pole. In the former, a knight on horseback would charge with his lance in combat position and attempt to pass his lance through a dangling metal ring only a few inches in diameter. In the latter skill test, a knight rode at a dummy warrior balanced on a rotating pole that had a shield attached to one wooden arm and a counterweight attached to the other. The rider had to be quick as well as accurate, for as soon as his lance hit the shield the dummy spun around and the counterweight would knock a slow horseman in the back of the head as he passed.

THE REWARDS OF A TOURNAMENT

A knight's performance at a tournament could generate a considerable fortune, especially for those skilled on horseback, in the form of captured warhorses, armor, and ransoms. The reverse, however, could also be true. Many knights established reputations as professional jousters and brawlers, touring all of Europe participating in one tournament after another. Some of the more successful knights were sought out as opponents because of the potential wealth one might gain by defeating them.

The day before the start of a tournament, combatants along with wealthy families pitched elaborate tents as temporary living quarters on the perimeter of the tournament field. One strategy for challenging opponents and possibly

❧ WILLIAM MARSHAL: ❧
THE QUINTESSENTIAL KNIGHT

Of all the courageous and chivalrous knights mentioned by medieval chroniclers, none was better known or respected for his fighting and leadership abilities than Sir William Marshal. He won more tournaments and battles in England and France than any other knight. Between the years 1170 and 1183, Marshal established his status as an undefeated knight in more than one hundred tournaments. It was during these tournaments that Marshal began to establish his friendships with the powerful and influential men of his day. His reputation and character were built through his own actions and abilities.

In 1187, Marshal's reputation for valor on the battlefield made him a favorite of England's King Henry II and he became the king's personal knight. Marshal also served as Henry's bodyguard, counselor, and ambassador. When Hen-

ry's son Richard I came to the throne, he recognized Marshal as a brother. Fulfilling the promise made by his father, Richard gave Marshal the heiress Isabel de Clare and all her lands in marriage.

According to modern historians, Marshal was a knight who used his prowess in causes that were honorable to the king as well as causes that advanced himself and his family. Marshal earned his rewards by his sword, his counsel, and his careful and prudent loyalty. His largesse was openly displayed with style to both his own men and family as well as to his opponents. Marshal's piety was practical and realistic; he founded priories and abbeys and gave to those that were in his lands, went on crusade to Cologne, and fought as a Knight Templar in the Holy Land. Marshal lived by a strong sense of loyalty and honor that perfectly balanced and complemented his prowess as a knight.

winning the most expensive equipment was for knights to advertise their willingness to fight by displaying their shields at the opening to their tents. Tournament participants took time to ride by all tents to assess the competition and the value of their shields and armor. Knights with the best armor could expect the most challenges.

Perhaps the most famous and successful knight was William Marshal, a man reputed to have captured and ransomed five hundred knights over his career. During one tournament, Marshal personally captured ten knights, ransoming them, all of their armor, and twelve horses. Marshal was willing to do anything to gain a ransom. He once stumbled upon a badly wounded knight in full armor whom he claimed for ransom. Marshal picked up the mangled man in his arms and carried him into a nearby tavern. Once there he presented the confused and wounded knight to his friends as ransom, saying to them, "Here, take him to pay your debts."[25]

THE TOURNAMENT BANQUET

As was the case with many displays of ceremony during the Middle Ages, wealthy knights were obligated to act as host and present elaborate and costly banquets following a tournament or joust. The French writer Jacques Bretel recorded in 1285 one such banquet after a tournament in Chauvency,

France: "Then the heralds called a halt to the tournament and the knights returned to the castle for the final feast, discussing who had won prizes, and grumbling if they had lost."[26] Win or lose, banqueting played an important role in the social life of knights, and how they were orchestrated revealed a great deal about those paying for them and those invited.

One of the main responsibilities for a knight organizing a banquet was determining the seating arrangement. Where each knight and his lady were seated was based on their social standing in the mind of the host. Those most honored sat closest to the host, with everyone else decreasing in importance as the distance between their seats and the host's increased. A salt cellar, a small silver container of salt, was placed midpoint on the very long banquet tables, creating a demarcation between those of the highest social worth and those with the least. Sitting "below the salt" was always considered disappointing.

Hunting and killing the meat and fowl to be eaten at the banquet was another job for the hosting knight. Main course meals often included exotic fowl shot in the knight's forest. Swans and peacocks were popular for banquets because they could be dressed as magnificent centerpieces, with their colorful plumage as decoration. Other popular but smaller birds included cranes, egrets, and quail. Favorite meat dishes including freshly killed stag, wild boar, and goat, all flavored by exotic imported spices. Guests ate their meats and other foods off trenchers, slices of stale bread that were used like plates. Following the heavier foods for those sitting above the salt, the blood-soaked trenchers were replaced by fresh ones to hold assortments of rare fruits from the East, such as figs, almonds, and raisins. On occasion, especially in the presence of a king, the host was responsible for providing one of his kitchen staff to taste a small portion of each dish to ensure it had not been poisoned.

Hosting an elaborate banquet was not possible for most knights. Most did not have sufficient wealth to entertain dozens of fellow noblemen and women. Some did not even have sufficient resources to outfit themselves properly in full armor and a horse. For this unfortunate group, known collectively as knights of fortune, wandering the countryside without a permanent home was the norm.

CHAPTER 6

KNIGHTS OF FORTUNE

During the latter half of the Middle Ages, maintaining a large army in the field became increasingly expensive. The costs of feeding horses and squires, maintaining equipment, and occasionally paying bonuses to knights to fight far from home forced kings and nobles to release many knights from their contracts. For knights whose sole source of income was war, prospects of peace were unwelcome, as the English mercenary Sir John Hawkwood noted when replying to two priests who had expressed their wishes for peace: "May the Lord take away your alms. Do you not know I live by war and peace would be my undoing?"[27]

These knights who relied heavily on fortune, or chance, to scratch out a living were called knights of fortune and were a common sight as they roamed the roads of Europe looking to ply their warrior trade in a variety of unorthodox ways. Many were seasoned combat veterans, while others were young and inexperienced. Even though most came from wealthy families, many of them were not firstborn sons and custom prevented them from inheriting their fathers' lands. This medieval custom, called the "right of primogeniture," gave inheritance of a father's land to the eldest son. All others departed the family estate as knights but rarely with more than a small bag of coins.

Some knights of fortune found legitimate, albeit unrespectable, work. However, the majority preyed on the old, the innocent, and the helpless. Their collective lot in life was disreputable in the eyes of most citizens, yet they managed to eke out a living nonetheless. The most common work available was fighting as a mercenary.

MERCENARIES

Times of peace were not kind to knights in need of war to make money.

Many knights openly expressed contempt for peace and willingly acknowledged that they knew little more than fighting, as is evidenced by one knight who candidly admitted, "Peace delights me not! War—be thou my lot!

Law—I do not know it save a right good blow to the head."[28]

Without a prolonged war to fight, many knights were unable to generate sufficient income to maintain their manor staff, warhorses, and weaponry. For some

An entourage of knights leaves the castle during peacetime. With no enemies to fight, knights lost their livelihood in times of peace.

✦ THE GREATEST MERCENARY ✦

The knight considered to be the greatest mercenary fighter was the fourteenth-century Englishman Sir John Hawkwood. He was a knight who made a reputation for himself in France, and an even larger one in Italy, as a feared mercenary. Many medieval writers considered him to be one of the greatest unrelenting killers on the battlefield.

Hawkwood began his fighting career as an errant knight who attained a great reputation after killing dozens on the battlefield. Later he traveled to Italy to fight as a mercenary. He fought for the princes of several great cities, such as Genoa, Bologna, Pisa, and Florence. Fighting for Florence earned him the incredible sum of 130,000 gold florins—the modern equivalent of several hundred thousand dollars and more money than any other mercenary had been paid.

As his fame for slaughter spread, he hired a band of knights to fight in his private mercenary army. These well-paid men were the terror of Italy, and other armies refused to fight against them. In 1375, Hawkwood accepted pay from the city of Pisa, which was intent on making war against Florence. Terrified of the outcome, the Florentines entered into an agreement with him, by which they agreed to pay him 30,000 gold florins in three months on condition that he agree not to attack them. He accepted the offer.

On his death in 1394, the Florentines gave him a public funeral of great magnificence and decreed the erection of a marble monument in the cathedral Santa Maria del Fiore in Florence. Although the monument was never executed, the famous Renaissance painter Paolo Uccello painted his portrait on the inner facade of the cathedral, where it can still be seen.

---

battle-tested, unemployed knights, their best option was to wander the country in search of work as mercenaries—warriors willing to accept money for fighting for a country or noble other than their own. From the twelfth century on, prolonged periods of sporadic warfare between local nobles necessitated the hiring of mercenaries. According to historian Maurice Keen, "There were sovereign princes at one another's throat everywhere: this indeed is one of the distinctive features of the period. One party to a quarrel could hardly abstain from employing mercenaries unless it could trust the adversary to do so too, which it clearly could not."[29]

One such well-known knight turned mercenary was the Frenchman Sir Bertrand, who while addressing himself to the Count of Poitiers offered his services to the count, saying, "I can help you. I have already a shield at my neck and a helmet on my head. Nonetheless, how can I put myself in the field without money? If you want us to remain with you, give us money."[30]

A distinction was drawn between knights who fought in the service of their lords and mercenaries who would fight for anyone. Many mercenaries who fought for foreign kings and nobles and pillaged their way across the landscape were despised as vermin. Keen makes the point that "the effect of the passing of men at arms under such leaders as Sir John Hawkwood [a mercenary] . . . resembled the passing of swarms of locusts. They stripped the land bare and human government proved powerless to restrain them."[31]

This equestrian portrait of Sir John Hawkwood was painted on the wall of a cathedral in Italy.

BRIGAND KNIGHTS

Knights down on their luck occasionally turned to the age-old profession of robbery. Although most knights were able to endure periods of unemployment during peacetime, a few knights forced to abandon their land became desperate. Setting aside their chivalric code of honor, these despairing brigand knights set out for Europe's highways in hopes of relieving travelers of their valuables, including money, jewelry, and horses.

Europe during the Middle Ages had developed a vast network of roads. These roads carried thousands of foot- and saddle-sore travelers from Rome as far north as Amsterdam and

London. Unfortunately for unarmed weary travelers, brigand knights might descend upon them, blocking their route unless money was handed over. Historian Walter Meller notes, "Robber knights rode down from their castles to ruin travelers on the roads, or shut them up in their castles to be held for ransom—such adventure was part of a knight's devoir [duty]."[32]

One self-confessed brigand knight tried to instill courage in his band of men by explaining that having the courage to rob will make them rich: "It will be a happy day. For we shall seize the usurers' [money lenders'] goods, and pack animals will no longer pass safely, or the mayor journey without fear, or the merchant on his way to France, but the man full of courage will be rich."[33]

JUDICIAL COMBATANTS

Occasionally knights accepted jobs representing other persons involved in disputes that could only be reconciled by what was called judicial combat. A lack of law courts and law codes meant that many disputes could not be reasonably resolved. In such cases, many European countries supported the use of combat to determine a person's guilt or innocence. Theological leaders reasoned that in a judicial combat that pitted two disputants against each other, God would intervene to protect the innocent party and vanquish the guilty.

Oftentimes, litigants unwilling or incapable of engaging in judicial combat were permitted to employ knights to fight in their place. Although this practice has the appearance of being the work of mercenaries, the medieval mind saw it quite differently. To them, knights were acting as the hand of God to reveal the innocent and the guilty persons. Judicial disputes became so common in England that during the reign of King Richard II, the Duke of Gloucester determined that all disputes in his territory had to occur in an arena prepared to his specifications:

> 60 paces long by 40 broad, the ground flat and hard, without large stones. It should be strongly barred (fenced) with exits at East and West, the fence of sufficient height to prevent a horse from leaping it. Lance, long and short sword, and daggers are permitted.[34]

Unemployed knights in need of money were eager to lend their services for a fee. When such an event was announced, the two hired knights faced off either on horseback with lances or on foot with full armor and swords. These combats were public spectacles attracting large crowds in search of entertainment. Some combats ended quickly with one well-placed lance thrust or sword blow, but not all did. The rules requiring these combats to commence at noon but not continue past sunset suggest that some were fought for several hours. Most, however,

A medieval tapestry depicts mercenaries robbing and murdering hapless travelers. Many mercenaries unable to find work turned to outright thievery.

ended when one contestant was either exhausted to the point of collapse, seriously injured, or in some rare cases, killed. However the contest ended, the custom did not allow an appeal.

During the twelfth century, chroniclers reported a dispute between two monasteries. Recognizing that neither dared allow their monks to resolve the dispute by fighting, each monastery hired a knight to engage in judicial combat. One unknown chronicler reported the following outcome of the combat:

Saint George slays the dragon and rescues a princess in this illustration. His legend epitomizes the chivalric life of an errant knight.

And when the champions came together to do combat, the injustice [done by the monks of Holy Cross] did not remain in doubt for very long, but was quickly revealed by the Lord. In fact the champion of the monks of Holy Cross and their allies was shamefully defeated and laid low without delay, and he thus acquired nothing else for the monks of Holy Cross save the highest shame and the greatest harm.[35]

Kings also invoked judicial combat to settle disputes. The English king Edward III, for example, once challenged the king of France to combat between one hundred knights representing each country in a *combat à outrance,* the French term for a battle to the death. The French king, however, chose to decline the invitation.

THE ERRANT KNIGHT

The errant knight, as the name suggests, was a wandering knight. Typically young, lacking battle experience, and short on money, the errant knight led a highly romantic gypsy existence wandering aimlessly across the European landscape. Intending no harm and revering the code of chivalry, these young men rode in search of fame and adventure.

The errant knight was easily differentiated from other knights by his old, dented armor, lack of a squire, and a horse that was typically too old for more successful and wealthier knights. The errant knight's life on the road was often filled with unusual adventures and dramatic suffering, as one young knight stated: "Armed with wood, iron, and steel, I shall endure heat, cold, frost; scattered meadows will be my dwelling-place. Discord and severity must serve the place of love-songs and I shall help the weak against the strong."[36]

Errant knights were famous for seeking a meaningful quest in their young lives. Part of their mystique was their sense of moral destiny to fight alongside a noble king, rooting out wicked and corrupt lords, or coming to the rescue of beautiful young women. Romantic as their lives might sound, the medieval historian Johan Huizinga suggests that such highly idealized notions of knighthood "were a cultural phenomenon that was becoming more and more divorced from the harsh realities of the period."[37]

In reality, knights roaming the countryside in search of food were a scourge to peasants and their land. The fourteenth-century lawyer Bartholomeo of Saliceto commented after seeing his countryside ravaged by errant knights, "What shall I say about those companies of armed men who overrun the territories of our cities? I reply that there is no doubt about their position, for they are robbers . . . and as robbers they should be punished for all the crimes they have committed."[38]

Errant knights occasionally provided practical service. They often served the needs of a lord and were welcomed into castles with offers to spend the night and have a free meal if they were willing to joust with local squires in need of experience or with seasoned knights in need of sharpening their skills. Customs in France promised them a good warm bed and meal if they won but a night's stay in the barn's hayloft with cold leftovers if they lost. On occasion, a noble might give an errant knight a specific military task to perform and pay him upon its completion, or he might offer him the chance to act as a bodyguard for the noble's traveling family.

KNIGHTS WHO FALTERED

Knighthood was intended to remain with a man for life, but circumstances sometimes caused it to be rejected or revoked. On occasion, a knight chose to reject his knighthood because the costs of arms, armor, horses, and retainers exceeded his ability to afford the costs. Those sons who did not inherit land when their fathers died also had difficulties paying for the equipment required of knights. For these knights, the job exceeded their financial abilities.

Beginning with the twelfth century, many men eligible by birth to become a knight opted instead to serve only as a squire, while some dropped their claim to knighthood altogether. To counter a rash of knights abdicating their once coveted and respected titles, England's King Henry II imposed a scutage that required those knights who opt out of military service to pay a tax, which in turn was used to hire mercenaries to serve in their places.

Knights also faltered in their obligations to uphold their oaths of chivalry. Each oath might differ slightly from all others, but all fundamentally required the knight to protect the church, the poor, and the helpless. Yet for knights desperate to remain employed, many quickly swept aside their oaths to carry out the warring orders of popes, kings, and wealthy lords.

Egregious violations of the code of chivalry could result in stripping a knight of his knighthood. On rare occasions a public rite was held on an outdoor stage where an offending knight was stripped

Knights and the Problems of Primogeniture

The custom of the right of primogeniture intended to keep land in one single family. In cultures where land was divided equally among all children or among all sons, the division of the land left each heir with so small a plot of land that it could not support one family, let alone pay for a knight's military equipment.

The right of primogeniture had its drawbacks for the firstborn knight as well as for any younger brothers. Although the elder son would eventually inherit all the family land and its wealth, he might wait a very long time depending upon his father's health.

Furthermore, few eligible women were willing to marry him until he began his adult life independent of his parents, which meant that some knights were old by the time they produced children.

The younger brothers in a family were unfortunate for different reasons. Some could stay and work for their older brother, but most were forced out of the castle with a very poor prospect of marriage. The life of an errant knight attracted few eligible women. A young knight forced to depart from a relatively wealthy family might receive a small amount of family money when he departed the village, but most were forced to find work elsewhere and few ever returned home.

of his armor, which was then broken into pieces and thrown at his feet while his spurs were removed and tossed upon a dunghill. His shield was tied behind a cart horse and dragged through the streets, and the tail of his warhorse was cut off. Wearing a cloth shirt, the knight was carried to a church on a litter like a dead body. There a burial service was read over him; since he had lost his honor, he was now symbolically looked upon as a corpse.

For those knights fortunate enough to have been firstborn sons, times of peace meant something very different than to their younger brothers. Due to the right of primogeniture, the eldest sons enjoyed the luxury and accepted the responsibility of returning to their estates to provide manorial administration.

CHAPTER 7

VILLAGE ADMINISTRATION

Knights did not spend their entire lives charging into battle, participating in tournaments and jousts, and thundering across the landscape while pillaging the poor. Most of their activities occurred in times of peace when they turned their attention to the management of their homes and estates to make them profitable enterprises. A knight's civic responsibilities, although not as colorful and exhilarating as his military obligations, were far more extensive, time-consuming, and varied.

To guarantee the smooth running of farms and businesses and to protect each vassal's interests, the knight kept a keen eye on all aspects of his vast holdings. And lacking central law enforcement officers, courts, or prisons, each knight upheld the law of the land.

DEFENDING THE HOMELAND

Of paramount importance to the villagers was the knight's obligation to provide protection for the village. This duty was always symbolized by the sword that was strapped to his waist wherever he rode. According to historian Norman Cantor in his book *The Medieval Reader:*

> Whatever else the aristocracy did—in politics, religion, art, and literature—it was military valor and personal strength and courage that had originally made the great noble families powerful in society, and this physical prowess was continually necessary to sustain their position in society.[39]

A knight's requirement to defend his villagers obligated him and all male family members to provide a safe haven at his personal residence for the villagers in the event of an invasion. He and his family were duty bound to take in all village peasants and provide mounted horsemen in full armor for the defense of the village. This responsibility was viewed as having the strength of a contract, and for that reason the lord of a village often pledged an oath to each subject, such as this one from the thirteenth century that promises to provide protection:

> It is right that those who offer to us unbroken fidelity should be protected by our aid. And since such and such a faithful one of ours, by the favor of God, coming here in

our castle, we willingly bear arms for those who have seen fit to swear trust and fidelity to us in our hand. Therefore we decree and command by the present precept that for the future this yeoman be counted with the number of antrustions [loyal followers guaranteed protection].[40]

Opening his home to villagers, whether it was an elaborately constructed stone fortress or a simple manor house, was a sacred duty to a

Villagers make merry during a festival, confident that their knight will protect them from all harm.

knight. He and his family made room by providing sleeping quarters, food, and fighting equipment for the castle's defense. Although the knight and his sons were military leaders, the villagers joined in with bow and arrows, clubs, and javelins. Following a successful de-

A group of knights demonstrates archery skills during a tournament.

fense of the castle, the knight would forgo the traditional collection of goods and services from peasants if crops and businesses were damaged by the invading army.

MANORIAL WAR GAMES

To provide adequate defense of the village, the knight took charge of training the peasant men in the use of weapons. On Sunday, following church services, he required all able-bodied men to meet for military training.

Archery contests were an entertaining way to hone villagers' accuracy with bow and arrows. Knights made straw-filled targets that were set up against the stairs or walls of the church. And the peasant men took turns aiming at the targets. As might be expected, archers took pride in their accuracy and contests were inevitable. To encourage further practice, knights rolled targets on wheels down lawns as the archers did their best to hit the moving targets. The lordly knight regularly offered small monetary rewards for the best archer.

Of equal importance to accuracy was distance and speed. Village archers practiced shooting at a forty-five-degree angle as far as possible and as rapidly as possible. Good archers were capable of shooting distances up to four hundred yards and were capable of releasing ten arrows a minute. Al-

ᘒ DISPENSING MANORIAL JUSTICE ᘓ

Knights exercised absolute authority within their domains. They heard complaints, determined innocence and guilt, and levied fines. This list represents some of the day-to-day complaints brought against people and the fines levied by the knight of Durham, England. The list is from the article "Extracts from the Halmote Court Rolls of Durham, 1345–83" at the Calvin College Web site, *located at www.calvin.edu.*

Billingham, 1364. It is enjoined upon all the tenants of the village that none of them grind his grain outside of the domain so long as the mill of the lord prior is able to grind, under penalty of 20s [$2.40].

Coupon, 1365. From Alice of Belasis, for bad ale, and moreover because the ale which she sent to the Terrar was of no strength, as was proved in court, 2s [$0.24].

Newton Bewley, 1365. From John of Baumburg for his transgression against Adam of Marton, in calling him false, perjured, and a rustic; to the loss of the same Adam of Marton 40d [$0.40], penalty 13d [$0.13].

Mid-Merrington, 1365. It is enjoined upon all the tenants of the village that none of them insult the pounder [thresher] while fulfilling his duty, nor swear at him.

Newton Bewley, 1368. From Thomas, servant of the same [Adam of Marton] for drawing his knife to strike John Smith, penalty 40d [$0.40], by grace 12d [$0.12].

though an army of one hundred archers might exhaust its supply of arrows in four minutes, it would be capable of raining down chaos on the enemy with a shower of four thousand arrows in a concentrated area.

MAKING THE ROUNDS

In his role as lord of the village, a knight's day began early by patrolling the village and its lands on what was known as "making the rounds." Saddling up his horse and strapping on his sword (but none of his armor), and occasionally accompanied by his steward who was his right-hand man, a knight conducted a general survey of the manor's woods, meadows, fields, and pastures. He then checked to see that such things as the oxen were yoked to plows early in the morning, the manure was properly spread across fields, the forests were free of poachers, and the sheep were grazing in the agreed-upon meadows. One English noble described a knight's responsibilities thus: "To cause the land to be sewn, reaped, manured and cultivated, and all the wagons and ploughs and cattle together with the sheep, lambs, hogs and all other head of stock there to be managed and tended as shall seem best for our profit."[41]

Following the rounds in the fields and woods, the knight rode into the village where his first stop was the most important, the mill. No commercial business in a medieval village was of greater concern to the knight than the efficient and honest operation of the mill. Without it, there would be no flour for the variety of breads made daily. Of greatest concern was the steady honesty of the miller who could, if he wished, easily cheat his customers. Millers had a reputation for stealing small amounts of flour or rigging the scales to underweigh sacks of grain. Suspicion ran so high within many villages that a commonly told riddle asked the question, "What is

The mill was central to village life, and required an honest and efficient administrator.

the boldest thing in the world?" and the reply was, "A miller's shirt, for it clasps a thief by the throat daily."[42]

Following his visit to the mill, the knight would visit the butcher's quarters to ensure all blood and entrails from slaughtered animals had been properly washed away. He also sniffed the air to make certain that no tainted meat was being sold. The baker's shop was the next stop where he inspected the bread for illegal additives such as sawdust. Sometimes bakers used additives to unfairly add weight to the bread. Finally the knight rode past all other shops looking for possible thieves or beggars.

Knights with large holdings were forced to hire, at their own expense, a handful of men to assist them in the administration of the village. Good advice in this regard was given in the thirteenth century by Walter of Henley, who admonished all knights, "Look into your affairs often, and cause them to be reviewed, for those who serve you will thereby avoid the more to do wrong."[43]

THE VILLAGE MILL

Administering the village flour mill was one of the most important responsibilities for a knight. Its wheel turned by water flow, the village mill ground an assortment of grains into flour for baking a variety of breads, dinner rolls, pie crusts, and cereals. The mill was the most expensive piece of village equipment because of the two massive, flat circular stones used to grind the grain and the gears that rotated the stones. For these reasons, mills were owned and controlled by the local knight.

The knight built his village's mill but rented it out to a miller who paid rent in exchange for charging locals to grind their grains. The cost to the miller was high; the knight took a percentage of all flour milled, called a multure. To pay the knight's rent and cover his own profit, millers kept between one-sixteenth and one-twentieth of the grain brought in for milling.

The miller hoisted the villagers' sacks of grain to a chute directly above the flat millstones and dumped them in. The chute fed the grain to the center of the two stones so that the seeds tumbled out between the two grinding surfaces. As the stones pulverized the grain, the flour spilled out onto the floor. When the milling was finished, the miller scooped the flour into bags, weighed them, subtracted his multure, and handed the rest to the customer. From his multure, the miller owed a percentage to the local knight to meet his daily quota.

COLLECTING QUOTAS

At the heart of the social and economic relationship between the knight of a manor and his peasants was his obligation to provide land and leadership in exchange for goods and services. Among the knight's most difficult jobs, yet an essential one, was to collect what was owed him, known as "collecting quotas." Each peasant had an annual obligation, depending upon his or her profession, to provide some sort of service or goods. Typically farmers owed food, shop owners provided whatever products they produced—shoes, weapons, furniture, candles, etc.—and housewives were obligated to spend a certain number of days cooking and cleaning at the knight's manor house or castle. Quotas rarely changed over time, so when a farmer owed six hens and eighty eggs each Christmas, chances were good that his ancestors had paid the same amount for many generations.

Most knights kept careful records of quotas. One of the best documented is the account for the village of Elton, England, in the thirteenth century. Records indicate deliveries made by farmers included bacon, beef, goats, chickens, eggs, apples, honey, beeswax, meal, cheese, rye, and barley. From craftspeople came such necessary items as plows, oxen yokes, hinges, traps, rakes, wood, ale, and tallow—animal fat used to make soap and candles. One unusual entry in the registry required a woman to give her knight or lord of the manor one flowering rose in June in return for her land. Labor in the knight's manor was also recorded and noted the number of days women worked, especially around important religious observances such as

Christmas and Easter. The records also indicate that a few peasants opted to pay money in lieu of the goods or services they owed.

Not all peasants voluntarily paid their quotas. The account from Elton has a section for those peasants "in arrears" who had defaulted in their annual obligations. This tricky predicament forced knights to act as enforcers toward delinquent tenants. Although peasants had few rights and most were poor, they were sturdy, independent workers willing to confront their masters if they felt wronged. Disputes arose and tempers sometimes flared. Records indicate that from time to time, knights out collecting their quotas were attacked by a band of peasants wielding clubs and throwing rocks. One fourteenth-century woodcut depicts a knight lying next to his horse surrounded by armed woodsmen. Beatings prompted many knights, especially those with large holdings, to hire collectors, called reeves, who received a percentage of their collections. Failure of a family to meet their quota frequently resulted in fines or a one-day punishment in the stocks, a wooden contraption with holes for the neck and hands that held offenders. Failure over a long period of time meant the loss of an offender's house and rights to plow the knight's fields or to work in his village.

DISPENSING JUSTICE

Prisons did not exist in the medieval village, although crimes of various sorts were common occurrences. Lacking the ability to lock up violators of local law and custom, one of the jobs of a knight was to dispense justice himself. At a time when few law codes existed, the local knight's word was considered law, and he determined the type of punishment for certain crimes. The knight of the manor or a jury of twelve landholders under his direction held ultimate resolution of all court cases, and no appeals were allowed.

Most legal hearings, called *hallmotes*, were held at the knight's great hall in the manor house or castle, although occasionally chronicles record that informal hearings were sometimes held out-of-doors under a large tree or in some well-known public location. Anyone wishing to bring a complaint did so, and the knight listened to both parties in a dispute, questioned them, heard witnesses, and rendered his verdict on the spot. This sort of justice was informal but had the advantage of being relatively impartial and swift, and fines were generally in keeping with the guilty person's ability to pay.

Crime in the village committed by locals usually amounted to relatively innocuous acts such as poaching game in the lord's forest, petty theft, trespassing on a man's land, disputes over boundary lines or maintenance of fences, vendors cheating customers, and occasionally violence usually linked to drunkenness. Crimes committed by outsiders, typically beggars, usually involved the theft of

A knight (center, bottom) listens to parties in a dispute. The knight's decision was binding in legal matters.

food or a few coins from a merchant's money box.

Typical is this case from the record books of the town of Elton, England:

"John Allot was convicted of carrying away the hay of Reginald, to the value of four pence which he will pay to the same Reginald before the next court convenes, fine pardoned."[44] On rare occasions, when the penalty handed out was for punishment, the guilty party was locked in the public stocks and given some number of lashes to the back.

OBLIGATIONS

One of the more costly obligations imposed on knights, which was understood by all to be part of their job within the hierarchy of medieval society, was that of entertainment. All knights, regardless of their rank, were required to entertain their lords when commanded, which on occasion might mean entertaining the king and his entourage for a week or more.

The arrival of a lord's entourage was rarely a happy event in the life of a knight. Depending upon the lord's rank and wealth, his group might easily include a few dozen people on horseback and in coaches. The knight was required to provide them with places to sleep and food to eat, as well as a stable to keep their horses. The great distances that nobility traveled meant their stays were lengthy; a one-week stay was not uncommon. Providing for such a swarm of people could easily cost a knight, even a wealthy one, nearly all that he had. To soften the financial blow, the knight passed on many of the costs for food to his peasants, who would contribute breads, cheeses, small game, and pastries. Historians working in the Eng-

lish city of Yalding discovered the menu of one such elaborate gathering of nobility in 1375 that "required the preparation of 6 oxen, 25 pigs, 45 sheep, 50 stags, 100 swans, 300 geese, 300 peacocks, and 4,000 assorted desserts that included pies, custards, and cakes."[45]

Bands of entertainers who traveled from town to town were hired by the host knight for the week. They performed after dinner for the adults and during the afternoons for the children. Evening favorites were jugglers, tumblers, musicians, comedians, mimes, and firebreathers—men who gulped mouthfuls of flammable alcohol and then exhaled it onto a burning stake that erupted into a fireball to the amazement of the guests.

THE HUNT

For a knight, the hunt was more than entertainment. Regardless of his wealth or the number of peasants required to provide him with annual allotments of food or services, a knight still had the obligation to feed his family and guests. In the forest, often off-limits to the peasantry because the large game animals were reserved for the hunt, the knight chased down food in the form of deer, wild boar, and occasionally bear. He was usually accompanied by several hounds that assisted him in the hunt.

The master of the hounds directed the chase. The hunt required the knight to perform exciting equestrian maneu-

The hunt combined work with pleasure, allowing the knight to hone military skills such as archery as he pursued his favorite game.

vers, such as jumping fallen logs, charging across streams, and crashing through thick brush. When the stag or wild boar was cornered, both hounds and knight moved in for the kill.

Sometimes hunting was dangerous for the knight. Dangers included falling and breaking bones, being accidentally shot by an arrow intended for the game, or worse. The wild boar was the most dangerous of all animals because of its razor sharp tusks and because it could suddenly turn and attack the men on their horses. "The boar slayeth a man with one stroke, as with a knife," said the unknown author of the fifteenth-century hunting treatise *The Master of Game*. "Some have seen him slit a man from knee to breast and slay him stark dead with one stroke."[46]

The hunt was one of those rare combinations of work and pleasure. While pursuing game across his private hunting reserve with friends and family, a knight also took account of the land—to estimate animal populations, to locate illegal snares set by poachers, and to gather a supply of deadwood needed for winter firewood. The French writer Olivier de Serres captures some of the practicality of the hunt in this sixteenth-century commentary:

❧ A GRUESOME HUNT ☙

A gruesome yet superb description of a knight's hunt can be found in the English novel Sir Gawain and the Green Knight. *Although the book is fiction, the description of the hunt is considered by historians to be one of the finest and most accurate for students of the Middle Ages. This excerpt is quoted in Andrea Hopkin's book,* Knights.

At the first sound of baying [of the hounds], the wild creatures trembled. Deer fled from the valley, crazy with fear, raced up the high ground—but were fiercely turned back by the ring of the beaters, who yelled at them savagely. They let the stags pass, with their high-antlered heads, and the fierce bucks as well, with their broad and flat horns; for the lord had forbidden that in the close season any man interfere with any male deer. The does were driven rowdily down the deep valleys. There you might see the rushing of arrows loosened from bows. At each turn in the wood, a shaft whistled by, bit deep in their hides with its very broad head. How they scream and they bleed as they die on the slopes, and always the hounds are hard on their heels. The hunters with shattering horns race behind with such ear-splitting cries as if cliffs had collapsed. The beasts that escaped the men shooting at them were all savaged and torn at the receiving points, carried off from the high ground, driven down to the streams. So skilled were the men at the lower points and the greyhounds so big, that they caught them at once and tore them apart, fast as men could look on, right there. The lord, filled with delight, on horseback, on foot, spent the whole day in pleasure till the dark of night fell.

The aim of hunting, which is a pleasant pastime, is connected to many benefits: it favors health, due to the fact that one has to get up early in the morning and exercise, and sobriety. Moreover, hunting tempers the spirit, making man patient, discreet, magnanimous, bold, and industrious. We should not forget that hunting supplies the table with precious meats. Finally, it allows us to check the land and hasten the work.[47]

As de Serres makes clear, the working life of medieval knights was one of considerable hardship. Far from the romantic Hollywood image of the knight in shining armor, most knights passed their entire lives hard at work defending and managing their villages and peasant populations. It was this dedication that defended Europe from foreign invaders and kept cultural traditions alive following the calamitous fall of the Roman Empire.

NOTES

INTRODUCTION: WHO WERE THE KNIGHTS?

1. Quoted in Andrea Hopkins, *Knights.* New York: Artabras, 1990, p. 18.
2. Quoted in "Knighting Ceremonies," *Chronique: Journal of Chivalry.* www.chronique.com.

CHAPTER 1: THE APPRENTICESHIP OF A KNIGHT

3. Quoted in Melville Grosvenor, ed., *The Age of Chivalry.* New York: National Geographic Society, 1969, p. 228.
4. Quoted in James Watson, "Apprenticeship and Nature," Harn Web Page. www.mailbag.com.
5. Quoted in "The Office of Squire," *Chronique: Journal of Chivalry.* www.chronique.com.
6. Quoted in "Founding of the Knights Templar." www. veling. nl/anne/templars.
7. Quoted in Walter Clifford Meller, *A Knight's Life in the Days of Chivalry.* London: T. Werner Laurie, 1982, p. 133.
8. Quoted in Meller, *A Knight's Life in the Days of Chivalry,* p. 44.

CHAPTER 2: EQUIPPING A KNIGHT

9. Quoted in Snorri Sturlson, *Heim-*

skringla—the Chronicle of the Kings of Norway, 2003. www.capnmac. com.

CHAPTER 3: THE KNIGHT AT WAR

10. Frances Gies, *The Knight in History.* New York: Harper & Row, 1984, p. 12.
11. Quoted in Anthea Boylston, "The Bloody Cost of Medieval Warfare," The Exiles. www.the-exiles.org.
12. Quoted in "Medicine in the Medieval World," SchoolsHistory, 2004. www.schoolshistory.org.uk.
13. Quoted in Hopkins, *Knights,* p. 153.

CHAPTER 4: CRUSADING KNIGHTS

14. Gies, *The Knight in History,* p. 35.
15. Quoted in Anne Fremantle, *The Age of Faith.* New York: Time-Life, 1965, p. 55.
16. Quoted in Fremantle, *The Age of Faith,* p. 54.
17. Quoted in Paul Halsall, *Internet Medieval Sourcebook,* "Fulcher of Chartres: History of the Expedition to Jerusalem," Fordham University, December 1997. www. fordham.edu/halsall/sbook1old. html.
18. Quoted in Gies, *The Knight in History,* p. 41.

19. Quoted in Gies, *The Knight in History,* p. 41.

20. Quoted in Paul Halsall, *Internet Medieval Sourcebook,* "William of Tyre: The Foundation of the Order of Knights Templar," Fordham University, December 1997. www.fordham.edu./halsall/sbook 1old.html.

21. Scott J. Beem, "The (Not So) Poor Knights of the Temple," Eastern Illinois University, 2003. www.eiu.edu/~historia/1997/knights97.htm.

CHAPTER 5: TOURNAMENTS

22. Quoted in Grosvenor, *The Age of Chivalry,* p. 225.

23. Quoted in Meller, *A Knight's Life in the Days of Chivalry,* p. 135.

24. Quoted in Hopkins, *Knights,* p. 104.

25. Quoted in Gies, *The Knight in History,* p. 90.

26. Quoted in Hopkins, *Knights,* p. 111.

CHAPTER 6: KNIGHTS OF FORTUNE

27. Quoted in Maurice Keen, *Chivalry.* New Haven, CT: Yale University Press, 1984, p. 227.

28. Quoted in Grosvenor, *The Age of Chivalry,* p. 203.

29. Keen, *Chivalry,* p. 230.

30. Quoted in Frances Gies and Joseph Gies, *Daily Life in Medieval Times.*

New York: Black Dog & Leventhal, 1999, p. 91.

31. Keen, *Chivalry,* p. 228

32. Meller, *A Knight's Life in the Days of Chivalry,* p. 104.

33. Quoted in Gies and Gies, *Daily Life in Medieval Times,* p. 91.

34. Quoted in "The Joust as Judicial Combat," International Jousting Association, 2000. www.theija.com.

35. Quoted in Paul Halsall, *Internet Medieval Sourcebook,* "Charters Relating to Judicial Duels, 11th–12th Century," Fordham University, December 1997. www.fordham. edu./halsall/sbook 1old.html.

36. Quoted in Meller, *A Knight's Life in the Days of Chivalry,* p. 130.

37. Quoted in Keen, *Chivalry,* p. 219.

38. Quoted in Keen, *Chivalry,* p. 228.

CHAPTER 7: VILLAGE ADMINISTRATION

39. Norman Cantor, ed., *The Medieval Reader.* New York: HarperCollins, 1994, pp. 3–4.

40. Quoted in E.P.Cheyney, trans., *University of Pennsylvania Translations and Reprints,* vol. 4, no. 3. Philadelphia: University of Pennsylvania Press, 1898, p. 27.

41. Quoted in Graham Nicholson and Jane Fawcett, *The Village in*

England. New York: Rizzoli International, 1988, p. 27.

42. Quoted in Gies, *Daily Life in Medieval Times,* p. 81.

43. Quoted in Frances Gies and Joseph Gies, *Daily Life in a Medieval Village.* New York: Harper & Row, 1990, p. 49.

44. Quoted in Gies and Gies, *Daily Life in Medieval Times,* p. 215.

45. "A Banquet Befitting a King," Yalding, 2002. www.yalding.com.

46. Quoted in Gies and Gies, *Daily Life in Medieval Times,* p. 68.

47. Quoted in Hopkins, *Knights,* p. 107.

FOR FURTHER READING

BOOKS

G.G. Coulton, *Life in the Middle Ages.* Cambridge, MA: Cambridge University Press, 1957. This book gives a view of the day-to-day life of people in the Middle Ages, including the knights. The book provides a specific focus on what life was like for all levels of society in a medieval village. Much of the information in this book comes from archaeological evidence and from a thorough reading of hundreds of historical texts.

Denise Dersin, *What Life Was Like in the Age of Chivalry.* Alexandria, VA: Time-Life, 1997. This is a wonderful book to browse through for students studying the Middle Ages in general and knights in particular. It provides concrete information about the role of knights in European society. The illustrations and their descriptive detail are excellent.

Genevieve D'Haucort, *Life in the Middle Ages.* Trans. Veronica Hull. New York: Sun, 1963. This work is intended to illuminate the day-to-day activities of the lives of people who lived during the Middle Ages. The author draws from primary sources to describe many of the mundane yet fascinating details and experiences about the lives of the nobility, knights, and peasants.

David Edge, *Arms and Armor of the Medieval Knight.* New York: Crescent, 1998. This book provides informative details about the history and fabrication of medieval armor. Full-color photos and prints of armor styles complement the text.

Anne Fremantle, *The Age of Faith.* New York: Time-Life, 1965. This book provides an excellent, readable account of Europe during the Middle Ages. Its focus is on the development of the Christian church, yet it highlights the role of the church in the lives of knights, the development of the code of chivalry, and the Crusades and their influence over Europe. Included in the text is an excellent collection of photographs and medieval art.

Brooks Robards, *Medieval Knight at War.* New York: Barnes & Noble, 1999. Robards provides a dynamic book that focuses on the knight at war. The author provides fascinating insight into the difficulties of waging war at a time when armor and horses determined the nature of combat.

Barbara W. Tuchman, *A Distant Mirror: The Calamitous Fourteenth Century.* New York: Ballantine, 1978. This superb history of fourteenth-century Europe by Pulitzer Prize–winning writer Tuchman is acclaimed as one of the great histories of this century. The book is an excellent read that provides many insights into the role of knights at that time.

Stephen Turnbull, *The Book of the Medieval Knight*. Boston: Arms & Armor, 1995. This book is an excellent history of knighthood during the late Middle Ages. It is filled with information about armor, architecture, heraldry, manuscripts, history, and art.

WEB SITES

Britannia (www.britannia.com). This Web site is an excellent repository of authoritative information about major topics of English history. It contains many links to the history of knighthood in medieval England.

Chronique: Journal of Chivalry (www.chronique.com). This Web site provides links to hundreds of topics explaining chivalry and the role of knights during the Middle Ages.

Internet Medieval Sourcebook (www.fordham.edu). The *Internet Medieval Sourcebook* is maintained by Paul Halsall of Fordham University and is organized by three main index pages, with a number of supplementary documents. Each individual section contains dozens of primary sources covering an array of medieval political, social, and economic topics.

Medieval History (www.historymedren.miningco.com). The Medieval History Web site provides links to pages covering all topics of medieval history with a strong focus on knights and their significance to Europe.

WORKS CONSULTED

BOOKS

Alan Baker, *The Knight*. Hoboken, NJ: John Wiley & Sons, 2003. This book traces the evolution of the knightly institution from the early mounted warriors of Charlemagne to the crusaders. Baker provides eight chapters, each of which highlights one significant aspect in the lives of knights.

Marc Bloch, *Feudal Society*. London: Routledge, 1989. Bloch's work is one of the most influential books on medieval Europe.

Norman Cantor, ed., *The Medieval Reader*. New York: HarperCollins, 1994. This book contains more than one hundred carefully chosen primary sources from medieval documents.

E.P. Cheyney, trans., *University of Pennsylvania Translations and Reprints*. Vol. 4. No. 3. Philadelphia: University of Pennsylvania Press, 1898. This volume is one of twenty-three that provide hundreds of translated medieval historical documents of interest to historians and students of history.

Frances Gies, *The Knight in History*. New York: Harper & Row, 1984. Frances Gies renders a straightforward and enjoyable history of the European knight with clarity and readability. After an introduction that addresses the lack of evidence concerning the knight's origins, the author surveys knighthood as it evolved through the Crusades and examines the effect of the church and of romantic literature on the behavior and status of the mounted warrior.

Frances Gies and Joseph Gies, *Daily Life in a Medieval Village*. New York: Harper & Row, 1990. This book gives a view of the day-to-day life of people in the Middle Ages with a specific focus on what it was like to live in a medieval village. Much of the evidence comes from the archaeological work at the village of Elton, England, which helps identify the villagers and nobility who lived there.

————, *Daily Life in Medieval Times*. New York: Black Dog & Leventhal, 1999. This book reproduces much of the work provided by the authors in many of their other books. It does, however, provide an excellent cross section of all social classes in medieval Europe, with emphasis on knights and their responsibilities.

Melville Grosvenor, ed., *The Age of Chivalry*. New York: National Geographic Society, 1969. This book is one of the finest illustrated books available for students. Clearly focused on knights and chivalry, it explores their role in medieval Europe as well as their origins and their demise.

Andrea Hopkins, *Knights*. New York: Artabras, 1990. In this survey of medieval knights, Hopkins examines the historical reality of medieval knights as well as the romantic images given to them. Her book covers the origins of knighthood, its effect on the noble class, the influence of the church, the knight at war and peace, and his decline and survival. Vivid photos of medieval artwork enhance the book.

Maurice Keen, *Chivalry*. New Haven, CT: Yale University Press, 1984. This book is an excellent academic work exploring the origins, influence, and significance of codes of chivalry and how the codes shaped the role of knights.

Walter Clifford Meller, *A Knight's Life in the Days of Chivalry*. London: T. Werner Laurie, 1982. Meller provides a superb account of the variety of responsibilities of medieval knights. He also exposes the dark side of their profession as sometimes desperate men who trampled on the homes and rights of peasants.

Graham Nicholson and Jane Fawcett, *The Village in England*. New York: Rizzoli International, 1988. Both authors provide an excellent history of more than a dozen English villages, investigating their social, economic, and legal institutions.

Helen Nicholson, *Templars, Hospitallers, and Teutonic Knights: Images of the Military Orders, 1128–1291*. Leicester, England: Leicester University Press, 1993. This work provides a comprehensive history of knight-warriors during the Crusades.

Peter Speed, *Those Who Fought*. New York: Italica, 1996. This book is an excellent anthology of medieval sources, translated into English, that portray the lives of medieval fighters. Speed provides a significant number of sources that focus on the institution of knighthood and warring knights.

Stephen Turnbull, *The Book of the Medieval Knight*. New York: Crown, 1985. This book focuses largely on the political history of British knights through wars in Scotland, the Hundred Years' War, and the War of the Roses. In-depth examinations of individuals, battles, warfare, and other aspects of knighthood are highlighted by numerous photos of artifacts, castles, and heraldic banners.

INTERNET SOURCES

Steven Alsford, "History of Medieval Ipswich," Medieval English Towns. www.trytelcom.

"A Banquet Befitting a King," Yalding, 2002. www.yalding.com.

Scott J. Beem, "The (Not So) Poor Knights of the Temple," Eastern Illinois University, 2003. www.eiu.edu. /~historia/1997/knights97.htm.

Anthea Boylston, "The Bloody Cost of Medieval Warfare," The Exiles. www.the-exiles.org.

Stephen A. Dafoe, "A Slaughter of Innocents," Templar History, 2004. www.templarhistory.com.

"Extracts from the Halmote Court Rolls of Durham, 1345–83," Calvin College. www.calvin.edu.

"Founding of the Knights Templar." www.veling.nl/anne/templars.

Paul Halsall, *Internet Medieval Sourcebook,* "Charters Relating to Judicial Duels, 11th–12th Century," Fordham University, December 1997. www.fordham.edu/halsall/sbook1 old.html.

————, *Internet Medieval Sourcebook,* "Emich and the Slaughter of the Rhineland Jews," Fordham University, December 1997. www.fordham.edu/halsall/sbook1old.html.

————, *Internet Medieval Sourcebook,* "Fulcher of Chartres: History of the Expedition to Jerusalem," Fordham University, December 1997. www.fordham.edu/halsall/sbook1old.html.

————, *Internet Medieval Sourcebook,* "William of Tyre: The Foundation of the Order of Knights Templar," Fordham University, December 1997. www.fordham. edu/halsall/sbook1old.html.

"The Joust as Judicial Combat," International Jousting Association, 2000. www.theija.com.

"Knighting Ceremonies," *Chronique: Journal of Chivalry.* www.chronique.com.

E.L. Skip Knox, "Courtesy," Boise State University. www.history.boisestate.edu.

"Medicine in the Medieval World," SchoolsHistory, 2004. www.schoolshistory.org.uk.

"Medieval Logistics," U.S. Army Quartermaster Corps, 2004. www.quartermaster.army.mil.

"The Office of Squire," *Chronique: Journal of Chivalry.* www.chronique. com.

"The Structure of Medieval Society," Sara Douglass, 2002. www.saradouglass.com.

Snorri Sturlson, *Heimskringla—the Chronicle of the Kings of Norway,* 2003. www.capnmac.com.

James Watson, "Apprenticeship and Nature," Harn Web Page. www.mailbag.com.

INDEX

PICTURE CREDITS

ABOUT THE AUTHOR

James Barter received his undergraduate degree in history and classics at the University of California at Berkeley and went on to study ancient history and archaeology at the University of Pennsylvania. Mr. Barter has taught history as well as Latin and Greek.

A Fulbright scholar at the American Academy in Rome, Mr. Barter worked on archaeological sites in and around the city, Etruscan sites north of Rome, and Roman sites in the Naples area. Mr. Barter also has worked and traveled extensively in Greece.

Mr. Barter resides in Rancho Santa Fe, California, and lectures throughout the San Diego area.